The Happy Wife
&
The Happy Mother

7 Easy Steps To A More Satisfying
Life With Your Family From
A Common Sense Approach

Kimberly Hart

authorHOUSE®

AuthorHouse™
1663 Liberty Drive
Bloomington, IN 47403
www.authorhouse.com
Phone: 1-800-839-8640

First published by AuthorHouse   8/3/2009

ISBN: 978-1-4389-9449-9 (sc)

Library of Congress Control Number: 2009905661

Printed in the United States of America
Bloomington, Indiana

This book is printed on acid-free paper.

This book is dedicated to my late uncle, Dr. Terry L. Pulse, who taught me that if I could dream it that I could achieve it and from whom I learned the value of character and compassion as well as the power of optimism and the belief that love is all we truly need.

I also dedicate this book to my husband who is and will always be the great love of my life, and to my children who will always be my grandest achievements in this life. I love you all.

Table of Contents

Introduction

I wrote this book as a tool for every woman regardless of her background, socioeconomic status, race, religion or politics who is dedicated to giving her family the very best she has to offer while not losing herself in the process. As wives and mothers we all face the same struggles as we cope with our daily family lives. My goal is to share my perspective as a wife and mother by offering examples of what I have found that have enriched my own life and that of my family. I have also included some pitfalls to avoid by sharing personal failures as well. The acceptance that there isn't anything fair or equitable in regards to being a wife or mother is the first step in changing the way we perceive our family lives. I believe that we can learn from each other by being open-minded to change. If something isn't working in your life then you must make changes in order for improvements to begin.

The terms "happy wife" and "happy mother" are not oxymorons. They are completely possible as long as you have a clear strategy for success. The one constant in life is that life constantly changes. Whatever can go wrong often does. The key to avoiding certain mayhem is by removing all of the variables that are within your control. Our existence is filled with peaks and valleys. There are lessons to be learned and shared with our families every day. You have to be willing to roll with the ebb and flow of life by letting go of your preconceived notions and unrealistic expectations.

Society has led us to believe that we can accomplish as many things at once as we so desire and be successful at all of them. We have been programmed to think that we can simultaneously complete a higher education, have a successful marriage, a successful career, pursue philanthropic endeavors, travel, keep abreast of current affairs while raising a family and somewhere in the midst of all of that find time to better ourselves in the process. If for some reason we aren't able to be successful at any one of the aforementioned, we are to assume that we are failures as women and a disappointment to the women who fought for our equality. Mathematically it doesn't compute. You cannot give 100% of yourself to everything you do all of the time. Therein lies the predicament... in what area of your life are you willing to sacrifice?

As a woman, you set the tone for the mood of your household. Be constantly aware of the power and influence you have over your family. Be excited about who you are and about the life you are living. My disclaimer is that I am not a psychiatrist, psychologist or counselor. The advice and tools that I offer are not based on textbooks or theories but rather on real life experience. Certainly, what might work for one person won't work for another. I hope to offer a different point of view that you can incorporate into your life that will help you to achieve the goals you have for your family.

Before you begin the reading I would like for you to take a moment and think of how you actually define success for your family. What are some areas that you feel could use some improvement? Are there aspects of your life that leave you feeling overwhelmed? What are the strengths of your approach and how can you build on those? These are the questions that I want you to keep in mind while reading the seven steps.

The steps outlined are ideas that can be tailored to personally fit your family. I offer suggestions for a back to the basics approach that will ultimately lead to a more fulfilling life. As a whole many families seem to have gotten off track because we have placed our efforts on things that weaken the fabric we have woven. I believe that happiness is a state of mind. Negativity and pessimism are contagious, like a disease. Optimism and hope are sorely lacking in our society. We each have the power to decide how our lives turn out based on the choices we make. Once you have completed the reading I hope that you will be motivated to look at your family in a new light and begin the journey that leads to your family's success. Good luck!

Make Your Husband And Marriage A Priority

Your marriage is the most sacred aspect of your life. It is absolutely something that you should never take for granted. Finding a partner to share your entire life with and be there for you is a miracle and a blessing. You should be grateful for the gift of your marriage every single day. Everyone wants to know that they are not alone to navigate the path of life. Nothing ever seems insurmountable if you have a partner beside you as a copilot. Think about all of the people in the world to choose from and realize that you chose each other.

The first thing to realize in marriage is that ALL IS NOT FAIR. Sometimes and often at different times each person will give more than 50%. Seldom is it ever a 50/50 split. While that may be ideal, it is unrealistic. There will be times when you will NEED more than 50% and hopefully during those times your husband will give generously to you. It is important to reciprocate when your partner is in need as well. For example, if your spouse is working extended hours in order to complete a project at work... BE SUPPORTIVE. Pick up the slack and realize that it is only temporary. Remember whom your spouse is working so hard for: YOUR FAMILY. Don't nag and don't put guilt trips on your husband.

That is selfish behavior which ultimately only undermines the success of your family and eventually leads to resentment. Remember that marriage is a partnership. Chances are there is probably enough pressure on your husband at work without adding to the stress that he is already feeling. Don't get me wrong; I'm not advocating the support of a workaholic. I believe that it is important to make your family a priority. However, if this is a common theme in your marriage, then you might need to renegotiate.

The art of renegotiating is simple when done correctly. The mistake most women make is putting off having an overdue conversation with their husbands about certain things they aren't happy with until they have reached a meltdown point. Women often keep silent while secretly hoping that things will magically just work themselves out. All the while they are harboring resentment toward their husbands who have absolutely no idea that anything is wrong. Over time resentment leads to anger that will ultimately cause a wife to lash out at her husband and lead to an argument that could have been avoided. Instead of expecting your husband to read your mind, set aside some time when the two of you can have an uninterrupted conversation. Everyone reacts differently to conflict, but it is important to at least start the dialogue.

In a non-attacking manner let your husband know that you feel there may be excessive inequity in your marriage. Be specific and be able to back up your feelings with examples. You cannot make blanket statements without proof. For example: don't say, "You're never home and I'm tired of having to do everything!" The most probable response will likely be, "I come home every day after work. When do you think that I'm not home?" If you reply, "I don't know. You're ALWAYS gone," then you might as well consider the conversation over. You have lost his attention because he will think you're being emotional and unreasonable.

However, if the real issue is that your husband works late four nights a week and is playing golf every Saturday while you are cooking, cleaning, running errands and carpooling the kids to football, soccer, ballet, etc.; therefore, leaving no time for you to have a moment's peace…then it is time to speak up.

Here is an example of how to have a constructive conversation with your husband. "Jack, I'm glad that you are able to play golf on the weekend and spend some time unwinding. I realize that is important since you have been putting in so many extra hours at the office. I know that you are happier at home when you are able to have some time to yourself. Lately though, I feel like because of your golfing and overtime at work, I 'm forced to work double duty with the house and the kids which leaves no time for me. Would you consider spending some time with the kids on Sunday afternoon so that I could take in a movie with my mom or go have a cup of coffee with Linda? Is there any way that you could work late two nights a week as opposed to four? It is important to me that we have dinner as a family as often as possible. I would really appreciate your help in allowing me to find some quiet time for me also. If that doesn't work for you then perhaps instead of golfing every Saturday maybe you could golf every other Saturday and we could take turns carpooling to activities. That would allow me some free time to get a manicure or to have my hair done. It's important for me to get away from the stresses of the household too."

Every family has their own circumstances and schedules; therefore, your conversation might be very different. The example I gave you is just a model. The point is to be honest with your husband about what you need without putting guilt trips on him. Most men are capable of having realistic conversations and truly care about their wives' happiness. Be open- minded to his suggestions and encourage his input. Work with your husband to find a way for the both of you to achieve optimum happiness within your home. Marriage is give and take.

Communication is one of the most important tools your marriage must have in order to be successful. It's important to remember that our lives and schedules change. Most people abhor change. However, what works in October might not work in May. That is what renegotiation is all about. It is keeping the lines of communication open with your partner and respecting each other's needs. Each person needs to be acutely aware of what the other expects in the marriage. You must be able to clearly map out a path to travel on together. This path will consist of what you both can and cannot live with in a partner. It should run the gamut and include everything. For example: know where you both stand and what you expect regarding religion, infidelity, sex, finances, child-rearing, education and lifestyles, etc. There shouldn't be any "unknowns" out there. They will eventually find their way into your marriage and throw a monkey wrench in everything if you and your husband aren't on the same page.

After you have successfully negotiated the terms of your marriage, here are some ways you can be supportive during those times when your partner needs more than 50%:

- Greet your spouse warmly and with affection when he arrives home.

- Don't bombard your partner about the day's problems as soon as he walks through the door.

- Send a nice email during the day to the office telling your husband that you are proud of him and how much he is loved.

- Have a filling, but simple meal prepared for your spouse upon his arrival.

- Draw a hot bath and light some candles to help your partner unwind after a stressful day.

- Most importantly, give him some space for a few minutes to let him collect his thoughts and freshen up and transition from "work" to "home."

If there is something important to discuss, try this approach…"Sweetheart, I have something that I would like to talk to you about once you are settled in and have had some time to unwind and clear your head." Your husband will appreciate your respect for his time and potential frame of mind. Hopefully your spouse will come to you with a more open mind and an open heart because you showed him that his feelings were a priority. The worst thing you could do is to make your home a place that your husbands dreads coming to at the end of every day.

Men often feel smothered or nagged by their wives due to constant complaining. Be aware of this and be considerate. Important discussions should never take place when either partner is in a frazzled state of mind. When you are talking to your husband, it is crucial that you are not talking AT him and that it isn't a one-sided conversation. Women tend to interrupt often or increase their volume especially when they are in the middle of a passionate conversation.

Conversation truly is an art form. If your days are spent talking with toddlers it can be difficult to form complete sentences when speaking to other adults, much less mastering the art of conversation. Toddlers interrupt and speak loudly to get your attention. Don't let this habit carry over into your marriage. Communication isn't you raising your voice to your husband and telling him how unhappy you are. Just because you've expressed everything that was on YOUR mind doesn't mean that the conversation is over.

If you don't let your husband express his opinion after you have stated your point of view then he will disengage from the discussion completely, leaving you even more frustrated. It is important to listen. You learn more by listening than you do by talking. Don't pretend to listen. Really focus on what your husband is telling you and ask him to go into greater detail when you need clarity on an issue. He wants you to understand him and he wants to understand you. He needs to be able to talk to you without you always crying or getting upset every time every time he expresses a concern. Removing barriers by respecting each other's opinions and finding solutions through communication is a healthy way to create a true partnership with your husband.

It is important to CONSIOUSLY think of your husband throughout the day. This may sound strange, but it's easy to let all of the outside influences around us consume our thoughts. It might be the laundry, meals to be prepared, children's homework projects, things to be completed at the office, an impending oil change or whatever might be on your plate that keeps you preoccupied. Make a conscious effort to think lovingly about your spouse during the day. Make a mental list every day of at least five things that you appreciate about your partner. On occasion share your list with him. Be grateful to have him in your life. It is also a good idea to let your spouse know the attributes he possesses that you love and admire in him. Never miss out on an opportunity to let those important to you know that they are loved and appreciated.

Don't make assumptions. We often assume that those closest to us know how we feel about them. Forget that way of thinking. Remember that actions always speak louder than words. If you love someone, say it AND show it! Be specific. For example, if your husband makes you coffee every day then you might say, "I appreciate that you have coffee brewed for me every morning when I wake up." Or, "Thank you for washing my car and having the oil changed. It made my week so much easier not having to worry about that." We all need to know that the little things we do are noticed and appreciated. Hug your husband often and hard. When you are in an embrace, rub your hands down his back and pat him lovingly. Let him know that you are really there.

Kiss each other passionately. It is one of the most intimate and loving gestures you can share with your partner. Who knows where it might lead? As silly as this might sound, have fresh breath. Look nice for one another. I realize this isn't always possible, especially after you've endured countless sleepless nights with a newborn for example. Don't forget to take pride in your appearance. I know this can be difficult at times, perhaps all of the time.

I am the mother of four children that range between the ages of thirteen to two. There is always drama on any given day. Honestly, the only time for me to have a shower is either at 5:00 am or midnight it seems. I knew I was in trouble when my housekeeper showed up one Monday and clapped her hands and cheered with genuine excitement for me because for the first time in months I didn't greet her in my robe! If you need to be in pajamas all day, and there are those days, at least make sure that they are clean and not tattered.

When you get up in the morning, wash your face and brush your teeth before you do anything else. Brush your hair and dab on some concealer and lip-gloss. Put a little perfume on your wrist before leaving your bedroom and bathroom to tackle the day. I know from experience that once you leave your "dressing room" it is almost impossible to make your way back there to freshen up. Inevitably, a million things will come between you and your good intentions. What you CAN count on is for FEDEX, UPS, your nosy neighbor; the PTA president and the minister's wife to all drop by unannounced and force you to answer the door wearing your robe, the remains of your toddler's breakfast on your sleeve with curlers in your hair.

I speak from experience! At least if you've made the effort to start fresh then you will have a much better day. Otherwise, it is like trying to go to the office in your bathrobe! My grandmother had a saying, "A lady never leaves the house without her lipstick and earrings." I never really understood what she meant by that until I was a mother. As silly as it sounds, I usually try to put on a little lipstick and some earrings…even if I'm wearing my pajamas all day. Somehow, I feel more put together.

Try to remember what it was like when you and your husband were dating. That feeling of anticipation doesn't have to fade into non-existence. Hold on to it and remember it. We often get so comfortable with one another that we feel like we don't have to "try" anymore. I'm not saying that it's bad to be comfortable with your spouse, just don't let it turn into complacency. I am innately aware that there are at least one hundred other women who would kill to be married to my husband! Every woman flirts with my husband; it doesn't matter what age they are. I've witnessed this phenomenon with women ranging in age from sixteen to sixty-three! I just remind myself that I am the one he is married to.

Sleep naked and sleep next to your husband. Hold each other and fall asleep in one another's arms. Make love often, even if you are tired. If you find that you are just too exhausted to make love at the end of the day then be open minded to making love at a different time of day. Wake up a little earlier in the morning and spend some quality time together before getting out of bed. It could be a great way to start your day.

Always be open to your partner's advances, even if you might not be in the mood. If you are open to your partner, it is much easier to "get in the mood" and get lost in one another.

Make an effort to make each other feel good. Ask your husband what he needs and wants from you and be open to giving him that. It is also important for you to tell your partner what you need from him. Don't be afraid to talk to each other. Nothing should be off limits or taboo. At the same time, it is important for your partner to respect those times when you aren't feeling well, whether it is due to pregnancy, illness, etc. You should also respect those times when your husband isn't feeling well either and romance isn't on his radar. Don't mistake that for rejection. Again, remember that communication is the key to happiness.

DON'T FANTACIZE ABOUT OTHER PEOPLE, FAMOUS OR OTHERWISE. I have heard therapists say that it is perfectly healthy and harmless to do so; I disagree. How can it possibly be healthy to bring another person into your bedroom other than your spouse? This is my opinion. Ask yourself this question: would you want your husband fantasizing about another woman? There should be no double standards in a marriage. Personally, I think it's a great idea to fantasize about your husband! Think of the wonderful experiences you've had together and some new ones that you could create.

Do something unexpected. You might try having candles lit in the bedroom and lie on the bed with only rose petals strategically covering your body when he walks in. Once you are alone, walk into the room wearing only his shirt and a pair of high heels. If that doesn't sound like it might inspire your husband, then try wearing only a cowboy hat and a pair of boots to bed! You might be surprised at his reaction. Research tells us that most men are visual. They can't help it...so give him something to look at AND to remember. Help him to create his own fantasies about YOU.

If you can't get away for a romantic weekend out of town, enlist the help of a grandparent or relative if possible. Arrange for you and your spouse to spend the night at a local hotel. Eat dinner in the restaurant at the hotel or order room service. Spend the next day in bed sleeping in, eating, watching movies and making love. If the hotel has a spa then book a couple's massage. You will return home reinvigorated, relaxed and closer to one another which will allow you to both be ready to tackle the week ahead.

This next segment is worthwhile sharing with your husband. I believe that it is just as important for a man to use these skills as it is for a woman. Plan weekly dates. They don't have to be "night" dates. Maybe it is a nice lunch once a week. Perhaps it is a leisurely walk in a park and dinner afterwards. The point is to make time to spend with each other that doesn't involve anyone else. Take turns planning the dates and arrange for a sitter. Send your spouse an invitation early in the week and require an R.S.V.P. Spend the week building the anticipation and excitement. Give each other clues about what to expect. Come up with themes for the occasion. For example, challenge your spouse to plan an evening for under $50. Be creative.

Research romantic spots in your city where you and your spouse could share a bottle of wine under the stars. Make a reservation at a restaurant that you know your partner has wanted to try. Buy tickets to a movie that your SPOUSE wants to see, even if it's not your first choice. Get dressed up for one another. Look forward to spending uninterrupted time together. Try to make a pact that you will NOT talk about the kids, the bills or problems during your date. Hold hands in the car. Hold hands while you walk. Take the opportunity to be closer to your partner by focusing only on each other. Talk about dreams and goals and tell jokes. Just enjoy the company of the one that you love.

Leave your spouse love notes in unexpected places. Some good ideas are: the car, his briefcase or wallet, her purse, the diaper bag, the bathroom mirror or a sock drawer. On occasion, mail your partner a love letter or a card. It will be a real "pick me up" to find something in the mailbox other than junk mail and bills. Sometimes, spray a little of your signature fragrance onto or put a "lipstick" kiss on your note for an extra punch. For no reason, just send flowers to your spouse or bring them home. I absolutely love it when my husband does that for no reason. It lets me know that I was on his mind while he was out shopping and that he wanted to do something nice for me. Over the course of the week, I am reminded of his kindness and love for me every time I look at those flowers. This idea isn't just for men. Women you can do this too! They are beautiful, fragrant and decadent. They evoke feelings of love and romance.

I believe that the most important thing that you can do for one another is to be kind. Unfortunately, we usually treat the people that we love the most, the worst. Why is that? Why is it that in the heat of the moment we sometimes say the one thing that we know will hurt the most? Don't say hateful things in anger that you can never take back. Whether you want them to or not, they last forever. Don't call each other names. Even if you and your spouse make up after a fight, it is difficult to forget the terrible things that were said. They often play over and over again in your head like a stuck record.

Don't keep score. Don't keep score about anything. If you are having an argument, don't reach back into the past and bring up something else. Nothing good ever comes of it. You will never resolve anything that way. It is a cruel and childish tactic that is often used to punish the other person and undermine the actual argument in order to hurt the other person's feelings. Especially if the person reaching back is the person at fault at that moment, they will want to shift the blame away from themselves and focus it on the other person. You will both feel bad when one of you brings up a past argument or situation. It only opens old wounds and makes the relationship regress.

It could also cause your partner to lose faith and trust in you. They might be reluctant in the future to talk to you about "real" or "difficult" issues for fear that you might bring up past grievances where they were at fault. When past arguments and situations are brought into the forefront, there is never any resolution to *any* argument. It is important to RESOLVE issues and MOVE ON. Otherwise, your partner will feel as though they aren't allowed to have hurt feelings in your relationship or to simply be honest about their feelings. When someone feels like they have to hold their thoughts or feelings inside the only thing it leads to is resentment. Past mistakes of one partner DO NOT give the other partner a "free pass" to wrong their spouse because they feel entitled to do so because they were wronged in the past.

Whether you are religious or not, I Corinthians of the Bible speaks beautifully of love and is applicable to anyone who is in a committed relationship. These are my favorite verses: I Corinthians 13: 4-8 "Love is patient, love is kind and is not jealous; love does not brag and is not arrogant, does not act unbecomingly; it does not seek its own, is not provoked, does not take into account a wrong suffered, does not rejoice in unrighteousness, but rejoices in truth; bears all things, believes all things, hopes all things, endures all things. Love never fails."

However, if you find that you are in a place with your partner where you feel that you cannot forgive them for a transgression or circumstance then you should consider getting professional help for your marriage. Otherwise, you will have no future with that person if you continue to hold on to those feelings. Hatred and resentment are emotions that leave little room in your heart for anything else. It is unfair to hold someone hostage to your grudge or to a debt that they could never repay. Who decides the statute of limitations on punishment or persecution?

Don't let divorce be an automatic "out" when things don't go according to your plans or when times get tough. In my opinion, that is a large contributing factor to the divorce rate in today's society. It is a mistake to go into marriage with the idea that if it doesn't work out you can "just get a divorce." Please don't misunderstand my perspective on divorce. Certainly, there are circumstances where divorce is the only option. Sometimes two people just are not compatible. There are instances where people don't show you who they truly are until you are married. That is why I believe that it is so important not to rush into marriage.

Make a pact with your partner that divorce isn't an option. Have an agreement between each other to always work out problems and find solutions. There is nothing worse than having an argument with your spouse and having them threaten you with divorce every time there is a problem. It shakes your foundation and thwarts any potential progress.

However, I think it is worse for children to see two people demonstrate a bad example of marriage than to stay married only for the sake of the children. The children don't learn constructive methods of solving issues or learn anything about a partnership. They often go into their adult lives poorly prepared to have healthy relationships of their own. I was in a bad marriage for over ten years with someone who was emotionally, verbally and sometimes physically abusive. We had three children together and I thought I was doing the right thing by staying for the sake of my daughters.

I thought that I was hiding the abuse from everyone by putting on a happy face and pretty window dressing. It wasn't until my oldest daughter who was nine years old at the time said to me, "How can you just let him talk to you like that? I hate the way he treats you, and you just let him." It was at that moment that I was awakened from the coma I knew as my life. I realized that if my children didn't respect me as a woman then they would never respect me as a mother and that I would have no credibility with them. I had been demonstrating to them what they DIDN'T want in a marriage. I left my husband of almost thirteen years and it was the best thing that I ever did for my kids. They learned that I had the courage to do the right thing for all of us and saw me fight to get back my self-respect.

I was fortunate enough to reunite with my childhood sweetheart who is the love of my life. We married and he took my daughters in as his own by opening his heart and home to them. He showed them that there are good and decent men in the world who respect women and treat them with kindness. We had a son together a year after we were married and formed a family of our own. In my situation, divorce certainly was the right thing to do.

There are also those circumstances in which you realize that the person you married is not at all the person you thought you knew. You might realize that indeed you are married to a complete stranger. Your husband might be hiding a secret addiction to drugs, alcohol, pornography or gambling. These behaviors can put you and your family at risk.

If you are in an abusive situation, whether it is physical or emotional, my advice to you is to GET OUT, especially if there are children involved. Children learn by what they live every day. If a child witnesses abuse, they learn to abuse and that it is okay to be abused. They learn to be afraid. A child's home should be a place of safety, not a place of fear. There is never an excuse to hit someone. If your spouse has hit you even once, they will most likely hit you again. It might not happen right away, but a line has been crossed.

Once someone has hit you, it can be difficult to ever trust that person again. If you say nothing, your silence has given them permission to mistreat you. Silence is submission. By staying, you have potentially put yourself in a very dangerous situation. If there has been violence in the home, I encourage you to call someone for help. There are professionals at your local Women's Shelter who can offer counseling and assistance. However, if you feel that your situation is dire and you fear for your life, please call the police.

I think society has created an "instant gratification" way of thinking in our culture that bleeds into all facets of our lives. It has certainly led us into dangerous territories such as teen pregnancy, STD's, drug abuse and crime as well as the credit, mortgage and financial crisis. People often don't think about "tomorrow" because they are so focused on what they can accumulate today. Society's ideas concerning marriage today fall into that trap. Little girls dream of their Cinderella wedding and give little thought to what happens when the honeymoon is over and real life sets in.

The truth is that we have to work, pay the bills and have "real" conversations about "real" issues. You need to be having those conversations with someone that you know, trust, love and can rely on. People can be so caught up in what everyone else is doing that they don't appreciate their own lives. I call it "the grass is always greener syndrome." Don't worry about what anyone else's lawn looks like. Instead, put all of your efforts into manicuring your own lawn. Of course, I mean "lawn" as a metaphor for your life and marriage. I say that because inevitably someone will send me a letter telling me that they took great care of their lawn and that it was the most beautiful on the block and it didn't improve their marriage at all!

What people don't realize is that we are all doing the very same things. We all look bad when we wake up, except for my husband. He is the exception to the rule. That man is handsome 24 hours a day! Time is in love with my husband.

He looks better with each passing day. For the rest of us, we wake up with morning breath and messy hair, we all go to the bathroom and we all get dressed each day the very same way. Even those airbrushed images of the uber-perfect people that we call "celebrities" must brush their teeth, eat and use the bathroom. Simply put, they are people too. The only difference is that they pay people to dress them and put on their makeup! They usually rotate partners as often as the rest of us rotate our tires. This hardly makes them role models for successful marriages.

When you are out in public, whether you are alone or with your spouse, don't look at other people and wonder what it would be like to be with them instead of your husband. Don't wonder how they would treat you instead of your spouse. Don't look outside of your marriage for companionship or friendship. Friendships require a lot of work. You get out of them what you put into them. I have personally found that it is tiring to keep up friendships with numerous people. You feel obligated to call or answer the phone whenever they call or to email regularly. There is also the added pressure of finding what precious little time you have to spend with people other than your family, whether it is having lunch, playing bunko or participating in numerous organizations.

I don't mean to sound jaded, but it has been my experience that a lot of effort can be put into pleasing other people that really don't improve the quality of your life. Quality friendships are rare. The truth is that most of the people in our lives are little more than acquaintances and offer mostly superficial things like gossiping and playing tennis on Tuesdays.

Don't look to someone or something else to fill a void that might be missing in your marriage. If you feel like there is something lacking then you should let your partner know and give them the opportunity to hear your concerns in order to fulfill your needs. Be careful when "reconnecting" with people from your past, especially if they are of the opposite sex. If someone whom you had a past friendship or relationship with suddenly finds a renewed interest in you it might be a bad idea to be in touch with them if the conversation becomes mostly about your spouse or your marriage.

DO NOT give someone else power over your marriage by showing any signs of weakness in your relationship. One of the worst things that you could do to your partner is to tell someone else your spouse's insecurities or the intimate details of your marriage. It is a betrayal. Over time those conversations eventually lead to your "friend" convincing you that you would be better off without your spouse.

Human nature is a very strange animal. It seems that most people secretly root for others to fail. It's sad but true. If that person had been such a good friend to you then you wouldn't have lost touch with them in the first place. Friends of the opposite sex are never a good idea. Period. Everyone has his or her own motives and agendas and no one will ever place as much importance on your marriage as you will.

While technology has improved our lives and bridged gaps that were once unimaginable, I fear that in some ways it has consumed our existence. Online gambling, online pornography, random Internet searching, MySpace and

Facebook are all potential marriage wreckers. I believe that it has taken over many people's lives in a negative way. For example, it's been reported that people are spending as much as 6-8 hours a day on Facebook alone! If this is true, then when are people working, caring for their children or spending time with their spouses? There must be an enormous amount of lost productivity due to the number of hours people are just logged on to Facebook.

Overall, I think the general concept of social networking is a good idea and an efficient way to share information with your friends and family. However, there is always a down side to something in excess. I don't think there is anything wrong with posting photos of your family and looking at photos of your friends and making nice comments. The problem is when your daily life begins to revolve around your time on Facebook or whatever your preferred social site is.

The reason that we call the past the past is because it is supposed to be behind us! Life has a natural order and balance to it. When what is supposed to be behind us suddenly thrusts itself into our present our equilibrium is thrown off. People from our past can collide with our life in the present. We sometimes look upon the past with nostalgia and through rose-colored glasses. Some of us harbor regrets and ponder what might have been if only we could go back and do or say something differently. The Internet provides us with a platform to communicate these thoughts as well as the confidence to say things we might not otherwise say because we don't have to communicate face to face and risk rejection.

It can be very flattering to learn that someone from your past had a crush on you that you were not aware of. However, these potential "confessions" to the people from our past whom we had crushes on or who had crushes on us have no legitimate place in our current lives. What do you do with that information? It is awkward, unnatural conversation and could cause you to look at someone less than platonically and vice versa. It isn't healthy to reminisce with someone regarding a past romance, even if the romance was only hoped for in the past. It can snowball into a full blown what if I wasn't married to my spouse scenario. Before you know it, you are consumed with the grass is greener syndrome.

I'll say it again... Friends of the opposite sex are never a good idea. Acquaintances are one thing, but "friends" are another. The last thing you need in your life is for another woman, regardless of how she looks, focusing her attention or affections on your husband, even if it is only through the computer. It is inappropriate for another woman to have an intimate conversation with your husband, especially about your marriage under the guise of "friendship" or in a flirtatious manner. It is also inappropriate for your husband to allow that type of conversation to persist. If he is open to her advances then he will become closed to yours, even if she lives 1500 miles away.

It would be just as detrimental to your marriage to have another man focusing his attention on you. You should also discourage any flirtatious conversation from taking place whether on the computer, at the office or wherever you might encounter someone. I make a point to behave the same way I would want my husband to behave if he were in my place, regardless of where I am. You should never do or say anything that you would be ashamed of your husband or your family to know about. It's that simple.

Marital predators, regardless of whether they are men or women, are all the same wolves dressed in sheep's wool. They are people who are bored with their own lives and find excitement in destroying someone else's. It most often starts out with flattery. If the predator is someone from your past then these conversations usually all start out the same way. They will tell you how great you look and that you haven't aged a bit. Soon after that they might confess that they had a secret crush on you and wonder if you felt the same way. That will usually lead to the "if I could only go back conversation." They will most likely try to get a snapshot of your life to see if there are any chinks in the armor.

They might even comment on your photos. Red flags should go up if comments from men are only about you or comments from women are only about your husband, rather than commenting on "your family." In that case, they are trying to size up their competition. These predators all operate the same way, especially women. They will make themselves appear to be the perfect person who has no faults and try to solicit information about your marriage such as any difficulties that might have occurred. The point is to make either you or your husband feel like you made a poor choice in your spouse and to realize that this person would have been the better choice. Eventually, they will try to determine the weaknesses of your marriage and offer a "sympathetic" ear. They are trying to plant a seed of doubt in the hopes that it will grow and flourish.

At some point they will suggest that you call them sometime because it would be so good to hear your voice… blah, blah, blah. They will usually give out their cell phone number; because of course they wouldn't want you calling their home number in the event that THEIR spouse might answer. They will then ask for your cell phone number for the same reason. If this happens even once, then a dangerous precedent has been set. They are testing your marital boundaries. If their intentions were honest, then they would have no problem calling your home number rather than speaking to you in a clandestine manner. What may start out as flattery can lead into dangerous territory. Who hasn't seen Fatal Attraction? Need I say more?

"Instant chats" with these predators or anyone of the opposite sex for that matter are the same thing as secret phone calls because your respective spouses will have absolutely no visibility to those conversations. Those "chats" are not saved and there is no record of how long they lasted or with whom they occurred. Keep this in mind… they know that as long as THEY are occupying your time, then you aren't spending it with your spouse. My guess is that if the predator realized that you weren't interested in communicating with them "secretly" because both you and your husband's computers were completely available to one another, not only would they and should they be embarrassed, they probably wouldn't be interested in communicating with you at all because it wouldn't be as exciting or forbidden.

You shouldn't be "friends" with former boyfriends. It's just stupid. Former relationships should stay exactly that… FORMER relationships. You should have absolutely NO communication with someone you have previously had any intimacy with. There should be no open doors to past relationships. There should be no double standards here. If either you or your husband is logging on to social networking sites then you both should have complete access to each other's websites, including friends, conversations and emails. You shouldn't feel the need to start closing windows on your computer whenever your spouse walks into the room if you have nothing to hide. You should both be keeping it clean and wholesome at all times.

I'm not trying to create problems that may not exist. I'm just trying to bring things to your attention that you might not be aware of. You should never grow complacent in your marriage. Complacency leads to boredom and boredom can lead to disaster. Humans can be tempted. It's your job as a wife to cover all of your bases and know who is in your husband's life personally, professionally as well as on the computer. If he isn't doing anything wrong then he will have nothing to hide and shouldn't become defensive in regards to his time on the computer.

The same goes for you. Your husband has the right to know about everyone in your life that you have any contact with. He should also have access to your computer and whatever email account you have, including all of your passwords. He should be able to look at your cell phone history or listen to your voicemails at any given time. He should be able to look at any credit card or bank statements or cell phone bills whenever he wants to. You shouldn't be hiding anything from your husband and he shouldn't be hiding anything from you. If either one of you are keeping a separate PO Box and separate credit card account or secret cell phone, then you are living a double life reminiscent of the infamous

Scott Peterson and you should consider the possibility that you need serious help.

People are spending all of this time communicating and reconnecting with people other than their spouses and spending less and less time with their partners. We have to honestly ask ourselves this question, "Do these people truly have an investment in our lives?" The answer is no. It is a pastime. It is like a fantasy where we can pretend to be someone else. It most often isn't real. People are putting their best foot forward on sites like MySpace and Facebook, almost like a "persona." People are usually only posting the most flattering photos of themselves and often exaggerating their accomplishments and possessions. It's like walking into your ten-year high school reunion where the only thing anyone seems to be concerned about is impressing each other. When you are communicating on these sites you often aren't discussing real things like the mortgage, sick children and science projects, which are the conversations that make a marriage less than exciting.

If either you or your husband are logging on to websites in order to engage in scandalous activity then it's no different than dialing up a 1-900 number and believing that the person on the other end is a gorgeous intellectual who has great conversation skills and understands your inner-most thoughts. Reality most often is that the person on the other end of the line is in the neighborhood of 300 plus pounds living in a dilapidated trailer park, wearing a bathrobe and hasn't shaved or bathed in over a month! People on sites such as Facebook rationalize this behavior by telling themselves that the people they are talking privately to aren't strangers because they knew them twenty years ago!

Don't allow this to spiral out of control. There is absolutely no harm in keeping in touch with new or past acquaintances through Facebook or whatever mode you communicate with people as long as a wholesome environment surrounds your conversations with no secrets from your partner. Just remember to use it in moderation and don't let it consume your entire life. Don't fall into this trap. Never let someone come between you and your husband.

If you are on a social networking site, only put out good things. Praise your husband for being a great husband and father. Use it as a platform to tell the world how wonderful he is. Only use the "private messages" for conversations that you don't want OUTSIDERS seeing, such as personal information about your family. "Outsiders" don't include your husband. If you type something that you wouldn't want him to see, then don't send it. If you feel the need to delete your email, then you should not be communicating with that person at all. Remember that you made a lifetime commitment to this person and remind him of the same. Find excitement and conversation with each other and never get sidetracked.

Here's a side note to keep in mind. Most men engage in less than wholesome vices because they are either bored or frustrated with their wives and their perceived constant "nagging." I'm not saying that it's their wives fault. This is often the excuse men use to justify such behavior. Don't make your husband punch a time clock. Treat him like an adult. Allow him freedom. When he is in his office or working in the garage keep the kids out of there and leave him alone. It's important for your husband to have his own personal space where he can work, think or just relax uninterrupted. Don't make unnecessary trips into his office or out to the garage to bring him something to eat or drink. Remember that he is perfectly capable of getting it himself. Otherwise, he will feel as though you are checking up on him and only resent you for it, even when all you are doing is making sure that he is comfortable. Women are nurturers by nature, but most of the time that is a trait that goes unappreciated by men.

Don't give him an excuse to "rebel" by looking at online porn or whatever the case may be because you won't let him play poker on Thursday night with his friends or let him go to the gym to work out a couple of times a week. If you allow the world beyond the walls of your home to become "forbidden," then your home will be the very last place he ever wants to be. You will be amazed at what he WON'T do if given the option to do what he WANTS to do. However, if backed into a corner, eventually all men rebel on some level.

Nothing in a marriage should be considered deviant as long as both partners are willing participants and it is solely between the two of you. It only becomes deviant when one partner is keeping a habit secret from the other. If that is the case then there is a breakdown in communication. For example, if your husband wants to look at online pornography then don't judge him and condemn him for it. Find out why he wants to look at it and what he is trying to get out of it. Find out where you can fit into the equation and be open minded to what he has to say. If he refuses to allow you into that part of his life then you might consider marital counseling because online pornography probably isn't the problem.

If you aren't happy with the way your husband is treating you, then tell him. Don't give someone permission to treat you badly. This is a two way street. If you sense that your husband isn't happy, then ask him why and what you can do to make things better. We can't read each other's minds. Tell your husband how you need to be treated and why. Listen to him when he explains his grievances with you, even if they are hard to hear. Ultimately, happiness and partnership are the goals.

When I am out in public, I find myself thinking of how lucky I am to be married to my husband. At the grocery store I think of him on every aisle. I think of things to buy that I know he likes and of ways to please him. I often visit the card aisle and pick up a card for no reason to give to him. I anticipate seeing him again. When you think like that then everyone else becomes invisible to you. There will be no temptation. Make your marriage the center of all of your thoughts and actions.

Don't lie to each other. Don't even tell small lies. There is never a reason to lie to your partner. I'm not saying that you have to be cruel. If your spouse has a chosen a shirt that is unflattering, but you don't want to hurt his feelings, don't lie to them. Be honest, but in a kind way. You could say, "I like that shirt, but I think this other one would look even better on you." No one will appreciate a response of, "You look terrible in that shirt." There is never an excuse to hurt someone's feelings. It takes a lot more effort to be mean than it does to be nice. I love The Golden Rule. "Treat others as you would have them treat you." It is so simple, yet so perfect.

Trust is everything. Even those small lies that we tell ourselves won't hurt anything always do. If you can lie about something small, then you can lie about anything. Talking honestly with your partner about circumstances that may be difficult will only make your marriage stronger and create a more solid foundation for future growth. Lies are like termites. They eat away at the heart of your marriage and destroy it from the inside out, even if you can't SEE it at the moment. Over time, your marriage will be ruined and there will be no foundation on which to build anything of substance.

One of the biggest mistakes wives make is talking about their marriages to other people. Your marriage is sacred. Your husband is sacred. You should never speak negatively about your husband or your marriage to anyone…not even your mother or best girl friend. Don't commit the cardinal sin of talking about marital problems with someone of the opposite sex. If you are having difficulty in your marriage, talking about it with others will only weaken it. No one else will ever care as much about your marriage as you or your husband. It is a strange phenomenon that I've seen time and again. Most people want the best for you unless it's better than what they have. Human nature is animalistic. It makes other people feel better about their own lives when they feel like someone else's isn't going so well.

Do you really trust someone who might not have your best interest in mind to give you sound advice? The only person that needs to know the intimate details of your marriage is the person that you are married to. Your marriage is between you and your husband only, without exception. If you speak negatively about your husband, then you have betrayed him. You should always lift him up. He should be the only person with whom your loyalty lies. There will certainly be times when he will make you angry or annoy you. You will do the same to him. Be his partner and be HIS best friend. Don't weaken your marriage by attacking the other half of it. Solve the problems, but with him.

Never argue in front of your children. It is frightening for a child to hear an adult argument. If a child is unfortunate enough to hear an argument, they are usually NOT fortunate enough to hear the resolution, which often takes place in private. A child needs to live within a cocoon of safety and stability; however, it can be can be acceptable for them to witness a disagreement. It's healthy for children to learn that we have different opinions and observe constructive ways to reach compromises. Be a living example to your children of what they might aspire to have in a marriage.

This next segment is also worthwhile sharing with your husband. Make a big deal out of birthdays, anniversaries, Mother's Day, Father's Day and Valentine's Day. Don't ever forget them or act as if they aren't important. These milestones in our lives are moments that are often taken for granted. Most of us would agree that as we get older there is less excitement about celebrating our birthdays. We associate our birthdays with aging and inching closer to our own mortality. I think that is a huge mistake! It is an opportunity to CELEBRATE the life of the person you have chosen to spend yours with. It is also an opportunity to honor your spouse.

I'm not talking about being extravagant or spending a lot of money. Remember how wonderful it was as a child to have balloons and a cake with your name on it and to look around and realize that all of those people were there to celebrate you? Whether you remember it or not or whether it ever happened, the result is the same...it is wonderful! As we get older we lose the magic that was our childhood and it is unfortunate. It is also unfortunate that we send such negative signals to our children about getting older. We should teach our children that life is a journey that we all go on that is enriched by our experiences and should be cherished, not dreaded.

If money is tight, a simple card will do. "It's the thought that counts" is not a cliché. It is absolutely true. If you can't afford to buy a card then try writing a love letter. It will be more treasured than a million dollar gift because it came from the heart and was penned by your hand. Birthday celebrations don't have to be expensive. Plan on a family dinner that includes a cake that says HAPPY BIRTHDAY and have some balloons for decorations. It also sends a message to your children that your spouse is important to you and that you are grateful to have them in your life. Encourage your children to make a homemade card or write a birthday letter that tells their parent how much they are appreciated. Those are gifts that last a lifetime and truly keep on giving.

Anniversaries are markers of your commitment to your marriage and to one another. If it is possible, take the day off of work and spend it together. Eat breakfast with each other and spend the rest of the day doing things that the regular workweek doesn't afford. Gifts are nice, but not necessary. If you are able to purchase your spouse a gift, then do so. However, if money is a problem, then simple gestures are appreciated. Make sure to say, "Happy Anniversary." Have a card to give to your partner that they can open for years to come. Share a meal alone and a bubble bath and a glass of something bubbly before going to bed. Treat your partner to a back rub or a massage by candlelight. Reminisce with your spouse the wonderful times or trips you've shared throughout your marriage. Rejoice in your success of overcoming hard times you've faced together. Celebrate your marriage and the miracle of sharing your life with someone that you love.

Mother's Day and Father's Day are both important occasions. Children love these days of celebration. They often make gifts at school that will be your most prized possessions. They are made with such love. One of my favorite gifts came from my oldest daughter who is now thirteen. She gave it to me when she was in four year preschool. It was a folded white piece of paper with a pink bow on top of it. This is what was written in it:

> " Dear Mom,
> This is a very special gift
> That you can never see.
> The reason it's so special
> Is, it's just for you from me.
> Whenever you are lonely
> Or even feeling blue,
> You only have to hold this gift
> And know I think of you.
> You never can unwrap it
> Please leave the bow tied.
> Just hold the box next to your heart
> It's filled with love inside!"

There have been many times when I have read that note and held it close to my heart. These holidays are wonderful opportunities to let your children know that you are honored to be their parent. They are also moments to let your spouse know that you are grateful to them for the gift of your children. Being a parent is hard and often thankless work.

I had a friend tell me that her husband didn't get her a card or do anything for her on Mother's Day and that it really hurt her feelings. I asked her if she told him that and she said that she did. What was surprising was his response. He said, "You're not my mother. Why would I get you anything for Mother's Day?" I was dumbfounded, as was she. My response was, "You might not be his mother, but you ARE the mother of his only child." I asked her if she gave him a card for Father's Day and she replied, "Of course." Her husband made her feel like the most important job in her life meant absolutely nothing to him.

Whether he meant to or not is beside the point. Now she dreads Mother's Day and feels like it has no meaning to her family. I told her that eventually her son would be old enough to make his own card for her and that would mean more than anything else in the world. I also told her that maybe her husband would grow to appreciate the role of her as a mother through the eyes of their son. It gave her little comfort because what she wanted was for her husband to tell her that he appreciated the wonderful ways she cared for their little boy. She needed his validation regarding motherhood. We are all raised differently and have different approaches to traditions. I encourage you to celebrate these occasions with your spouse and start traditions with your own family.

Valentine's Day is what most men consider a "manufactured holiday", unless you are lucky enough to be married to a romantic man who actually looks forward to it. Why look at it that way? Look at it as an opportunity for romance! Every woman secretly wants chocolates, flowers and a card from her husband, even if she says she doesn't. Let's get to the point. Chocolate is fattening, flowers die and cards are overpriced. Who cares? It's a day devoted to love. Husbands...bring home a box of chocolates and a bouquet of flowers and give your wives a mushy card. Take her out for a romantic dinner, even if it's pizza over candlelight. Exchange gifts. It doesn't have to be extravagant. Here is a fun idea: buy each other pajamas, underwear or lingerie. Wear it for one another. Wives...send your husband on a scavenger hunt that ends with him finding you in bed wearing only a bow. Perhaps you might send him a singing telegram, a box of cigars or whatever he might like. The point is to do something. Be creative and celebrate the love you have for each other.

The most important thing in a marriage is not to take each other for granted. Our lives can change in an instant. We think that we have forever but we don't. Tomorrow is a gift, not a promise. Car accidents happen as unexpectedly as illness does. If you talk to a widow or a widower and ask them what they regret, most people often say the same thing. They would give anything to have just one more moment with the person that they loved and lost. Never let a day go by that you don't say, "I love you" at least once. Never part each other's company on bad terms.

When your husband leaves your home give him a hug and a kiss every time without exception. Tell him that you will miss him while he is gone and mean it. Let his last impression of you be one of love and tenderness in case it is the last time he sees you. Live each day together as though it might be your last. Each day we have is a gift. Don't leave things unsaid or undone between each other. Be thankful for every single day that you wake up next to your husband. Start each day with the thought, "What can I do to make his life better today?" By asking yourself that question and putting it into action you will be making your own life better. Give to him what you wish to receive. Be an example to him of love, fidelity, trust and commitment. Let there be no double standards. No exceptions. Think before you speak and then speak with love.

Adjust Your Attitude

My husband told me that the Marine Corps have a mantra that everyone should incorporate into their lives: "Every day is a holiday and every meal is a feast!" He said that he truly felt that way during his service to our country because he really believed it. He explained that it was a state of mind and that it was impossible NOT to be grateful when you approached every day like that. Ronald Reagan was quoted as saying, "Most of us spend all of our lives wondering if we ever made a difference. The Marines don't have that problem."

Be grateful for all things large and small that you are blessed to have in your life. So many women focus on what they can get, what they feel they deserve or what they don't have rather than wanting what the already have. Let's be honest, what do we really need? Instead of being envious of the car that Susie Smith drives, be thankful for the one that is parked in your garage. Appreciate your home and everything and everyone in it. When you begin to change your way of thinking, your perspective about everything changes.

The more grateful you are for what you have, the less you continue to focus on what you do not have. Each new realization will reveal new blessings in your life. Don't measure the success of your family by someone else's standards. Learn to be content. Teach your children to be content. Lead by example. If you are always competing with someone else for happiness, you will inevitably come up short. It doesn't matter what material possessions you have, there will always be someone with a larger home, a more expensive car, nicer clothes or belong to a better club, etc...no matter who you are.

Don't get stuck on that treadmill that goes nowhere. That way of thinking is a waste of productivity and it teaches your children to be shallow and judgmental. Encourage your family to focus on goals that actually lead somewhere. Children learn more by the examples you set for them every day than they do by what they are told. "Do as I say not as I do." That is a ridiculous cliché to expect a child to respect, much less follow. If a child hears you using foul language then they will use it too. Remember that children become adults. What kind of an adult are you raising?

Eleanor Roosevelt said, "No one can make you feel inferior without your consent." That single quotation sums up an entire attitude. Most of the time when people put on airs they do it to overcompensate for what they lack in confidence. Confidence is a state of mind, not the accumulation of possessions. If you know that you are doing the very best job of being a wife, mother, daughter or whatever role(s) you play in your life, then you have every reason to walk with your head held high...wherever you go.

Don't mistake arrogance for confidence. Confidence is quiet self-assuredness, not outward bragging. Confidence is not believing that the rules do not apply to you. Most of the time those people are the first to complain and the last to conform. True confidence is putting a smile of your face every day because of what you know and feel inside. That beauty radiates from within and shines brightly for all to see. Inner beauty is more attractive than anything you could ever wear on the outside.

I get so frustrated with the assumptions made by people that if a woman doesn't work outside her home, then she is ignorant, lacks ambition or is a lady of leisure. There is nothing leisurely about being a stay at home mom. I assure you that there is no more difficult job on the planet! It is a 24 - hour a day job with no break time, sick leave or paid vacation. There are no promotions to aspire to. There are no luncheons held in your honor. It is a rare occasion when someone praises you for a job well done. Did I forget to mention that the pay is miniscule? The obvious reason women stay home is for job satisfaction. It is a sacrifice for a woman to choose to stay home and raise a family. Most critics seldom take the time to see it from her point of view.

Once a woman makes the decision to stay at home she gives up many dreams that she had for herself, at least in the foreseeable future. She places the emphasis on her family and her home rather than on herself. While her contemporaries are competing in the workforce, she is busy scheduling appointments, changing diapers and doing the laundry. Her life is not glamorous, although it is rewarding. She gives up conversation with adults, working lunches and seldom is able to catch up on current events because toddlers shouldn't be watching the news on TV. Instead she becomes familiar with preschool shows and schedules play dates for children.

Any woman who has had to manage a home and a family is probably more qualified to fill a position in any Fortune 500 company than most people on the payroll! She has experience being the Human Resources VP, Chief Financial Officer, Chief Operating Officer, Office Manager, Conflict Manager, Computer Technician, Maintenance Supervisor, Head of the Accounting Department as well as the VP of the Strategic Planning Committee. However, if she were to walk into a corporation looking for employment she most likely would be told that she lacked current skills to compete in the workplace.

Mothers often underestimate the influence that they have on their children. Have you ever observed little girls playing together in preschool or kindergarten? They behave like miniature versions of their mothers. Your daughters are paying attention to everything that you say and do. By listening to your phone conversations with your girlfriends criticizing what some poor soul had the nerve to wear to the Jones' party and other meaningless gossip, they also learn to gossip, ostracize and to unfairly judge their peers. I am amazed at how early the catty behavior begins.

If you really want a good laugh and to prove my point, drive by any private school parking lot and observe the carpool line a few minutes before dismissal. You will see women getting out of their expensive luxury SUV's and sedans wearing their designer clothes and accented with a lot of jewelry and perfectly coiffed hair. They make their way from one car to another pretending to have a conversation with the occupants who don't get out. The truth is…it is a parade. They simply want the other mothers to see how fabulous they are. Now here is the really funny part. When the children are released, the mothers on the cell phones are oblivious and the mothers who are in the carpool fashion show don't want their children to hug them because they are made up so carefully that they might wrinkle.

One of the worst things I witnessed was when a mother in a car in front of me was so busy talking to another mother standing outside her window that she actually ran over her own daughter's foot as she was trying to get into the car because she wasn't paying attention! What's worse is that the mother was so oblivious she backed up over her daughter's foot; therefore, injuring her own daughter twice! I had personally observed this phenomenon for almost nine years while my daughters attended private school. It is utterly ridiculous yet rampant. How proud those children must be. There are a few mothers whose children attend private schools who aren't caught up in the "game," they are just the ones everyone else is talking about.

Keep your circle tight...very tight. Keep your neighbors at arm's length. There is absolutely nothing wrong with being private. The less people actually know about you and your family then the less truth they have to gossip about. Everyone wants to know and feels entitled to know everyone else's business, even if they just live next door to you. It is with absolute certainty I can tell you that the drunken, flirtatious divorcee down the street who is the proverbial damsel in distress and in need of constant handholding will air her dirty laundry in the hopes that you will do the same. The moment you walk out her door she will be on the phone to your next door neighbor telling her everything that you just said and making it sound even more salacious!

Your next-door neighbor will smile and pretend to be friendly until she fears that your husband might be more successful than hers. She and the widow across the street will become best friends at your expense and she will let out her yapping dogs every time she sees you and your family outside just to annoy you! That is until you call the Property Owners Association and force her to comply with the covenants regarding animals that are a nuisance. You think I'm exaggerating? The point is to exercise extreme discretion because people are strange and their behavior is even more bizarre when someone becomes jealous!

Equality is something very few people in the world actually practice. Your children should observe you treating the doorman the same way you would treat the President of the United States. One of the things I love the most about my husband is the way he asks EVERYONE he comes into contact with how their day is going. If we go to a restaurant, he asks our server if their day is going well. He usually follows that remark with a compliment. For example, he might tell them that they are doing a great job or that their hair looks nice. Everyone, no matter who they are, needs to hear a kind word every day. Remember that the kind word you share with a stranger might be the only kind word that person hears all day. It is amazing how well people respond to kindness.

I am amazed at the lack of civility in our society. Why is it so hard to hold open the door for a woman with a stroller? Is it such an inconvenience to smile or to say please and thank you? We are all humans sharing this planet. There is no one single group that is superior to another, regardless of what we have been told. Money doesn't buy class. It has certainly been my experience that the people who brag the most usually have the least to offer and they know it! My grandmother used to have a saying. She said that if someone had to constantly tell you how great he or she was then they must not be so great. No truer words were ever spoken.

I've seen first hand over the years the endless parade of the wannabes. They think if they drive the right car, wear the right clothes, send their children to the right schools, wear the right watch and belong to the right organizations, then everyone will believe that they have arrived. Who do you think they are trying to convince, everyone else or themselves? Those are the people who are in debt up to their eyeballs and become morally bankrupt as well as financially bankrupt. The truth is that the people who REALLY have something going on or have REAL wealth would rather just fly under the radar. They don't have anything to prove and don't feel the need to act important because they know that their success is legitimate.

If you really have a resume then you don't feel compelled to give your resume to everyone you meet. My husband has a motto that he lives by: "Speak softly and carry a big stick." Enough said. I can't think of a better example for our son to live up to as a man. He will teach our little boy that a man isn't a loud braggart; those are the actions of an insecure coward. He will teach him that a man has the confidence to let those around him make fools of themselves while he himself is secure in his silence. Abraham Lincoln believed that it was, "Better to remain silent and be thought a fool than to speak out and remove all doubt."

I have laughed many times over the course of our marriage at this very example. My husband has shown tremendous restraint around braggarts. My husband has amazing credentials that he would never tell anyone about. For example, he is an expert motocross racer, a Marine, professional pilot, chemist, mechanical engineer, successful business owner and inventor who holds numerous patents and trademarks. I list all of these achievements for a reason. I'm going to cite a couple of instances of living a life with grace and class while those around you exhibit none.

My husband bought a motocross bike and the girls and I ATV's to ride at a track where we got a membership. We parked our truck and unloaded our trailer. It hadn't been five minutes before some eighteen- year old punk slid his truck next to us and sprayed us all with dirt. Keep in mind that my husband was the only male in sight. The punk sprayed three little girls and a pregnant woman with dirt! We were so impressed. He then proceeded to tell my "amateur" husband how to ride his brand new bike and cautioned him about the speed. I watched in horror as all of this unfolded. The entire time my husband just kept his cool and thanked the young "man" for all of his helpful information. My husband then put on his gear and took off on the track like he was Ricky Carmichael. It wasn't long before people were pulling off left and right just to watch. He had the whole track to himself! No one even wanted to ride at the same time he did because he was so skilled! No kidding!

The following week we went into the local Yamaha shop where we bought the bikes. The owner, Roger, is a friend of my husband's. When we walked through the door the owner just laughed out loud. He said, "I heard that you got some advice on how to ride your new bike last week!" My husband replied, "Whom did you hear that from?" Roger said, "From the moron who was giving it to you! He said he felt like an idiot when he saw you ride. I told him that you had been riding for over twenty-five years. The kid said you were amazing and he wished you had told him what an expert rider you were. I just laughed and said that you would never say anything like that and THAT'S why people respect you. I told him that I hoped he learned his lesson."

Another example was when we bought our house and were going to take our children out on our new boat for the very first time on the lake. Everyone was so excited. Of course our next-door neighbors who are twice our age were convinced that my thirty-nine year old husband didn't know anything about a twin-engine boat. My husband patiently listened to them pontificate and said nothing. It was our oldest daughter, who was eleven at the time, who finally spoke up and said, "My dad flies jets at over 600 mph; I think he can drive a boat!" To put this in perspective… these people are beyond obnoxious with their condescension. My husband would have rather our daughter kept her silence and just let his experience speak for itself. Personally, I thought it was great. Needless to say there hasn't been very much neighborly interaction since then.

Everyone who meets my husband loves him. Women wish they were married to him and men wish they WERE him. He is charming and charismatic. I absolutely adore him. He is tremendously kind and considerate to EVERYONE. He has been that way since the day I first met him when he was seventeen. He is sincere and that is what people respond to. He has the ability to make people feel better about themselves. What I have found is that most often people want to make others feel badly in order to feel better personally. People usually describe him as the nicest person they ever met. I would have to agree! Imagine if we all aspired to have people say that about us!

Our son wakes up every morning with the same proclamation. He says, "Good morning, it's a beautiful day!" He believes it and he expects it. Every day is a gift. We should expect the best from each day and from ourselves. We shouldn't let our mistakes define us or our circumstances define who we become. There are so many things that are beyond our control. What we can control is the way we respond to our environment. It is never too late to be what you could have been. My husband says that all the time and I believe it.

With a positive attitude most everything else just falls into place. I am amazed at the depth of character my eight year old daughter demonstrates. While riding in the car recently she said, "Most things just usually work out the way they are supposed to." She is such a bright shining little light. She is flexible and optimistic and is capable of seeing the best in everyone. I have learned a lot from her about life. I have learned that worry is a useless emotion. Nothing productive ever comes of it. If we put our energy into a positive direction every time we feel the need to worry, we will accomplish so much more than just fretting about things that we have no control over. Take control of those situations and turn things around.

Invest In Your Children

Sometimes being a mother can feel like the most thankless job on the planet. When I start to feel this way I remind myself that being a mom is a "long term investment" and that I will reap the dividends down the road by reinvesting rather than just cashing out! Investing in your children is like creating a portfolio. You must be well diversified and cover all aspects of your investment. You have to plan for the unexpected and above all, exercise patience. It's important to remember that you are planting seeds for future growth.

If you are fortunate enough to be a stay at home mother, then realize this very important fact: You must be present at ALL times with your children. I don't just mean physically present; I mean emotionally present. The moment they get into the car after school or walk through the front door, they are full of information. This is the best chance you will have to get that information that is on the tip of their tongues. However, if you are on the cell phone or off in la la land, then you will surely miss it. Good luck getting them to spill the details of their day later. When you finally decide that you have some time to talk, they probably are no longer interested. Whenever a child is dismissed upon their arrival, they will often punish you by withholding what they know that you want from them... INFORMATION!

They will want to hurt your feelings the same way that you hurt their feelings.

Your eyes should light up every time your child walks into the room. They need to know that they are important to you. If they are made to feel like they are a burden, then they will learn to fell badly and place undue blame on themselves when something goes wrong. Showing your children love is as important as saying you love them. It's been my experience as a mother that the best time of the day to truly connect with your children is before they go to bed. It is a magical time when they are more calm and open to your parental influence. Make a habit of being a part of their bedtime routine, no matter what their ages are.

I have four children ranging in ages from two to thirteen. They all need me in a different way each day, but the point is they each need me. It is a good idea to stagger bed times if your children are spread out in age. Here is an example of a typical evening in our household. After we have all pitched in to help clean up after dinner, we all go our separate ways. I encourage my husband to do something just for himself whether it is riding his motorcycle, catching up on some reading or whatever helps him to unwind and relax. He always puts everyone else's needs before his own and I think that it is very important for him to focus on his needs as well. I send my 8, 10 and 13 year old children to their rooms to prepare for the next day. They are in charge of packing their homework into backpacks, replacing dirty gym clothes with clean gym clothes, choosing an outfit for the next day and gathering papers that require my signature. If they are taking a lunch rather than buying it in the cafeteria, then they make their lunch and place it in the refrigerator. After they have taken a shower, they read for approximately thirty minutes or until we come in to say good night.

This is also a good time to decide what everyone will be having for breakfast. I have very strong opinions about children eating breakfast before school. I think that it is a key factor in having a successful day. No one can learn properly if they are hungry. Even if your child isn't hungry at 7:00 am, they will surely be hungry before the lunch bell rings. I grew up with a single mom who had to work; therefore, my brother and I were on our own for breakfast most of the time. I would have loved for my mom to be able to make breakfast for me every day, but it just wasn't an option. I suppose that I carried that desire into my adulthood. It has been my experience that I tend to overcompensate with my own children in areas I feel were lacking in my own childhood. Breakfast is a key example.

I used to make these ridiculously elaborate breakfasts that were fit for a king. If someone wanted waffles, then I made waffles. If someone else wanted blueberry pancakes, then I made blueberry pancakes. If someone wanted scrambled eggs, then I made scrambled eggs. Sides of bacon, toast and fresh fruit and juice accompanied waffles pancakes and eggs. I put a lot of effort into preparing a wonderful breakfast for my daughters. The problem was that they couldn't have cared less! They sat there and stared at the food sitting before them. They ate a couple of bites and the rest of my hard work ended up in the trash!

My husband patiently watched this scenario unfold for months after we were married. Finally, one day he said something. He said, "Have you ever tried just putting a ball of foil in front of them for breakfast instead?" He suspected that the result would be the same. One morning I decided to test his theory, so I placed a ball of foil on a plate at the table for each of my daughters. As he suspected, the result was exactly the same. No one touched their food and just sat there for fifteen minutes. The only difference was that my middle daughter asked for seconds!

I realized that cereal, frozen pancakes, toast, fresh fruit or yogurt were completely acceptable as breakfast options. It didn't make me less of a mother to not prepare a gourmet breakfast. The point is for them to have something nutritious in their tummies before tackling the day ahead. I ask the night before what they want so that in the morning we don't need to have a conversation that they aren't capable of having at 7:00a.m. As soon as they are dressed they come downstairs and eat their breakfast with no drama. Everyone's day starts off well, including my own.

While my older children are preparing for bed I am getting my two year old into his bedtime routine. Routines are important because everyone knows what their roles are and what to expect. There are no surprises. Bedtime routines signal the end of the day and the importance of preparation for the day ahead as well as the importance of reflection and relaxation. After my toddler has his bath and brushes his teeth, we sit in a rocking chair and read together for twenty minutes or however long his attention span lasts. We say prayers together and talk about what our expectations are for the next day. I listen to what is on his mind and enjoy that special time with him. I make sure that he knows he is loved and important to us. He gets tucked in nice and snug and falls asleep under glowing stars displayed on his ceiling.

After my toddler is fast asleep I make my way upstairs to check on the progress of my older children. I start with the youngest and work my way up. I review and help with homework; sign all necessary papers and make sure backpacks are packed up. I also review their choices regarding the next day's outfits. The time to make necessary changes is not in the morning when you are trying to catch a bus or trying to get to school before the first bell. It's important to give your children some independence and learn what their own individual "style" is.

However, realize that motherly input is still required. If you are experiencing some difficulty with this remember that their peers will usually reign in those odd choices. For example: when my oldest daughter was in Kindergarten she was determined to wear a particular pair of leggings under her dress. I expressed my disapproval; however, I realized that there was a bigger lesson to be learned. I allowed her to wear something that looked absolutely ridiculous and let her make her own decision. The teacher just smiled upon my daughter's entrance into her classroom and said, "Good morning. I see that you dressed yourself today." She gave me a wink and I was on my way. I picked my daughter up at the end of school and asked how her day went. She looked at me and said, "Why did you let me wear these stupid leggings with this dress? They don't match." I reminded her that I did tell her that they didn't match but let her make her own decision. Her comment made me laugh. She said, "I guess those leggings weren't such a great idea after all." She knew that I had given her the freedom to make a choice, even if it was the wrong choice. She also learned that perhaps Mom sometimes knows what she is talking about.

While I am spending time with my eight year old I quiz her over spelling words and vocabulary, etc. Sometimes she still likes for me to read to her, but most of the time she reads to me or prefers to read independently. We listen to her latest favorite music and talk about her day and what is on her mind. She is also a wealth of information regarding her older sisters. They tell each other a lot of things and assume that their youngest sister isn't listening. Sometimes the youngest daughter can point me in the direction that my older daughters need me to go or she might provide me with clues of upcoming conversations. She likes to fall asleep listening to classical music so we turn her CD player on and the lights off.

I then make my way to my ten year old daughter's room. Information is a little more difficult to coax out of her. A nice segway into that conversation is to ask her what their class wrote about in their journals that day. Ten-year-old girls are fickle. Every day begins and ends with a different best friend. The catfights start so early! I have found that it is very important not to trivialize whatever crisis might present itself each day. To her it is extremely important. As her mother it is my job to give her the tools to handle adversity. Honesty is always the best policy. Don't give a standard line of "Everything will be fine tomorrow." It just might not be fine tomorrow. We role-play different scenarios of how to handle certain situations with her peers. I also let her know that no matter what happens at school she can find comfort and love waiting for her at home.

Another way that I have found to connect with my ten year old is to cook with her in the kitchen. Our hands and eyes are busy while the conversation is going on. She feels free to talk and to listen if we are busy at the same time rather than staring at one another. I never start the conversation with a "heavy" topic. I get her comfortable talking first about other things and then transition into more important issues.

I still make sure that my ten year old has brushed her teeth, flossed, washed her face and completed her bedtime routine before I leave. She likes to read for about thirty minutes before she falls asleep. I believe that it is important to teach our children to learn to unwind and relax to signal to their bodies the end of the day. Those habits will last a lifetime if they are enforced from an early age.

One of the life lessons I have taught my daughters is the importance of taking care of themselves. I am a stickler for clean hands and neatly manicured nails. Whether you realize it or not people will judge you based solely on something as trivial as the appearance of your hands. If you have dry hands and ragged nails, one might assume that you place little emphasis on your well-being and that you lack attention to detail or are sloppy in other areas also.

Brushed hair or styled hair is also important. As a mom I worry about my daughters with longer hair getting lice at school. Fortunately for us it hasn't happened. The school nurse gave me some great advice. She told me to add tea tree oil to their shampoo and that it would minimize their risk of getting it. There isn't a mother in the world that wants to deal with that nightmare! If you have a daughter with long hair, it is a good idea for her to wear it in a ponytail or wear braids to school. Jackets and bags are often in very close proximity to one another; therefore making the spread of lice a distinct possibility regardless of your family's personal hygiene practices.

I make sure that their clothes are not wrinkled and that they are clean. If my daughters want some of their laundry done before I am doing it, then they each know how to separate their clothes and operate the washer and dryer themselves. It is important to notice when your son or daughter needs to start wearing deodorant and then make sure that they wear it daily. Sometimes it can be a real struggle to get your child to take a shower every single day. They simply don't understand the need to do so. For them it is just an interruption in their day. They would much rather play XBOX or watch TV. Healthy habits start at an early age and it's your job as a parent to enforce those habits so that they will last a lifetime.

My husband is a stickler for healthy teeth. He wants the children to understand that good dental hygiene will benefit them for the rest of their lives. He also wants them to understand that poor dental hygiene can lead to numerous health problems throughout their lives. He has a phrase that I love, "You don't have to brush all of your teeth, only the ones you want to keep."

On occasion I will draw them a bubble bath in each of their bathrooms, light some candles and put on relaxing music. They think it is a wonderful treat. I hope that they will remember to take care of themselves when they are older by pampering themselves from time to time.

I finally make my way to my oldest daughter's room. I usually find her at the computer, listening to her iPod, with the TV on while texting her best friend. The first thing I do is to start shutting off all of her technology. I am trying to convince her that she can not possibly focus on any one thing while engaged in so many at the same time. I have found that it is very important to be aware of WHAT kind of music she is listening to. We have rules regarding explicit lyrics... they aren't allowed! We also have a rule that it's lights out at 9:00 p.m. I usually sit on the edge of her bed and ask about school projects and sports activities. She is very good about giving me details regarding bus behavior and conversation, which shocks me daily.

We talk about the gossip going on in school and her perception of it all. The most important tool I have found to communicate with her is this: no matter what she tells me, I don't act shocked or mortified, even when I am. I manage a calm demeanor and panic in private. This was the best advice that my aunt gave to me. Her daughter is now twenty-seven and they have always enjoyed a wonderful relationship. They talk daily and have very open lines of communication. My aunt was able to counsel my cousin as her mother, yet respect her opinions or choices even if they were different than her own.

My aunt told me that there were many times that she simply couldn't believe what her daughter told her. Her response was always the same. She remained a very cool exterior and simply tried to gauge her daughter's emotional barometer. She welcomed dialogue and offered advice and opinions without being judgmental. Her daughter grew into an amazing woman whom I respect tremendously. She has also played a very pivotal role in the lives of my children. Therefore, my aunt must know what she is talking about!

After the lights are out upstairs, I put whatever backpacks need to go into the car and make sure that my oldest remembered to put her bags by the door in order to be prepared to catch the bus. It is worth spending ten extra minutes in the evening to prepare for your morning because those calm ten minutes turn into a frantic thirty minutes the next morning. If you and your children start the day full of stress and anxiety then it makes it almost impossible to have a good and productive outcome. I make it a point not to have serious discussions in the morning that can wait until the evening. Do everything within your power NOT to upset your children or provoke tears before they go to school. Those emotions last the entire day.

We are still working out the kinks of what my husband calls "goodnight drama." Inevitably, after the lights are off upstairs and the doors are closed each of the girls takes a turn coming down stairs for that one last goodnight or glass of water. Bless my husband's heart... he had a reverse osmosis system installed upstairs in the wet bar for the girls to get their water each night; therefore, eliminating the need to make one last trip to the kitchen each night. The goal is to have everyone say goodnight to Dad at the SAME time BEFORE they go upstairs. Like I said, it's a work in progress and nothing is ever perfect.

Here is my favorite time of the day: MY time alone with my husband. After the goodnight drama has abated I am finally able to relax with my husband. I have found that I don't care what we are doing as long as I am with him. It's nice to simply watch a program we have recorded, enjoy a cup of coffee together or just talk about what is going on in our lives and how to make sense of it all. The truth is this... I look forward to being close to him physically and emotionally. I care to hear what he needs to improve the quality of his life and he is always open to my needs as well. I love the way he smells and just laying my head on his shoulder with his arm around me is all I need to be happy.

It is so important for your children to see that you make time for your husband and your marriage. They need to understand that a marriage doesn't just "happen." It takes work, but it is work that is worth the effort. Children often compartmentalize life in general by only seeing your role in their lives as that of the mother. However, by allowing them to see you actively participating in the role of wife, partner, friend and helper to your husband they are learning by example of how to have a healthy relationship with a future spouse.

Although my parents divorced when I was only two years old, I was fortunate enough that they shared no animosity for one another throughout my entire life. My stepmother is an amazing woman and I am so grateful to have her in my life. I can't imagine a more perfect partner for my dad. She recently gave me some wonderful advice. She said that it was important to set aside some time, even if it was only ten minutes, every single day that I truly connected with my husband. Her belief is that there is nothing more sacred than looking into your partner's eyes and letting them know that nothing is more important than the love you share. Even if you were to lose every single possession, as long as you have one another then nothing is impossible. You simply put one foot in front of the other and take life day by day. What a wonderful insight to share with your children as well as to demonstrate by example.

My husband and I have a policy with our children that nothing is off limits as topic of conversation. They are welcome to come to us with anything that is on their minds and we do not judge them. The wonderful man that I am married to is the kind of dad that we all wished that we had growing up. He is handsome, intelligent, educated, soft spoken and wise. No matter what questions our kids come up with, he has the answers. Forgive me for bragging; he's amazing. The point is that he is emotionally present and makes sure that our children know that he takes them seriously. Because he treats them with respect, they also respect him.

My husband and I also make a point to talk to our children at dinner. Everyone is supposed to take a turn telling the group about their day. We keep the TV turned off and we don't answer the phone. We eat in the dining room and make it an event that everyone is present at. This is still a work in progress. We are still working out the kinks of interrupting one another and lowering our volume. We call it the interrupting cow syndrome. Here's the joke: "Knock. Knock. Who's there? Interrupting cow. Interr ... MOO!" Whenever someone interrupts someone else, we simply say, "Moo." For some reason our eight-year old has this recurring problem of needing to excuse herself at least seventy-eight times during the meal to refill her glass or use the ladies room, and that's just the tip of the iceberg!

It's important to remember that small gestures make a big impact, especially with children. They need to know that they are loved more than anything else. Each of your children will need your expression of love for them in different ways. Even the teenager needs to know that they are loved whether they know they need it or not! There are many little things that you can do for your children that are little reminders that you love them and that you are with them even when you aren't together.

I always write my children a note each day to pack in their lunchbox. It's like a hug from me in the middle of the day. I keep it simple but poignant.

> Have a great day! Good luck on your math test! I am so proud of you and I think you are doing a great job. I look forward to seeing you when you get home from school. Thank you for being such a wonderful person. I love you very much!
>
> Love, Mom

My daughters have saved all of the notes I have written them over the years. I honestly didn't realize what an impact it made in their lives. I'm so glad that they have a tangible piece of my love for them that they can pull out whenever they need to hear a kind word from me, even when I can't be there. I also make a point to put a card from me in their bags whenever they have to travel somewhere so that there is always a piece of home with them wherever they go.

When my eight year old daughter was four we read a book together titled, The Kissing Hand. It is about a mother raccoon giving her little raccoon the courage to go to school and be away from her the entire day. She kisses the palm of her little one's hand and tells him to place it on his cheek whenever he feels like he needs a kiss from her. This gives him the confidence he needs to be away from his mother for such a long period of time. My daughter will occasionally ask me to kiss her palm before she leaves for school or spends the night with a friend. I love that I can do something to make her feel better when she is away from home.

We also have another routine that we practice whenever we are apart. We both look at the moon at exactly the same time and say good night to one another. It's the next best thing to saying good night in person and it makes us feel close to each other.

Another idea is to write a note on a blank piece of paper in your child's notebook or spiral where they fill find it the next day. For your older children who are consumed with technology you might send them an unexpected text message during the day to let them know that you are thinking of them.

It is important to try to make some "alone" time with each of your children whenever possible. In the spring I allow my daughters to each take one "sick" day toward the end of the school year. I take that opportunity to spend the entire day with them. We drop the others off at school, have breakfast together, and eat lunch somewhere fun; either take in an early movie or go paint some pottery. We spend the day just enjoying one another's company and the luxury of not being in our normal routine.

Another great idea is to have lunch with your children at school. I pick up my thirteen year old from school on Fridays and take her off campus for lunch and bring her back for her afternoon classes. It is only for 30 minutes, but it's time that we both look forward to spending with each other. Having lunch with your elementary children gives you a complete snapshot of your child's world. It's important to see how they interact with their peers and with whom they are spending their time. It's also important for the faculty to see you on a regular basis and realize that you are involved in your child's education from all perspectives, rather than just the PTA meetings.

One of the biggest advantages you will ever have as a parent is knowing with whom your children are friends. Allow them to have their friends over to your home on a regular basis and observe them interacting with each other. If your home is the one where your child and their friends are hanging out then you will always know where your child is and what they are doing. That gives you a lot of control over the social choices your children will be making.

Encourage your kids to invite their friends over for dinner regularly and to have sleepovers. You will learn a lot about your child through conversations with their friends. They will mention names and events that you weren't aware of. They will give you insights into what conversations you might want to pursue with your children at a later date or what to be looking out for as potential signs of trouble.

One of the biggest mistakes parents make with their children is overindulgence. You are doing your children an injustice if you give in to every whim because you want to give them what you didn't have. We have all been guilty of this at one time or another. The best gift you could give to them is to teach them how to live in the real world by giving them tools to succeed in it. If you are giving them everything that they want without teaching them to earn things then you are presenting a skewed perspective of the world and setting them up for certain failure.

I'm not saying that you shouldn't give your children things or indulge them on occasion. It's human nature that if we are given everything that we want at the moment that we want it then our expectations become unrealistic and we learn not to appreciate anything. If our children want a big-ticket item then it must be put on a birthday list or Christmas list. Otherwise then they must put a substantial amount toward the purchase. It's difficult to expect a child to respect things that they have little or no investment in. Nothing frustrates me more than seeing a bunch of junior high students treating the property that their parents bought for them as though it means nothing at all.

Last Christmas, my husband bought our oldest daughter the latest and greatest iPod. She wasn't expecting such an extravagant gift and was beyond excited about it. I told her that I didn't think that it was a good idea for her to take it to school because I worried that it might get lost or stolen. I was right and that's exactly what happened two months after she got it. She was devastated and didn't tell us for a long time. When we finally learned that it had been stolen I told her that we weren't going to replace it. If she wanted it replaced then she would have to use her own savings to do so. She thought about it for a few days before deciding that she wanted to get another one. I can say without a doubt that she takes better care of the one SHE purchased than the one we bought for her. She learned a valuable lesson about budgeting and responsibility.

It's never too early to teach your children about money. It shouldn't be considered a taboo subject that we can't discuss within our family. I'm amazed at the lack of information that our children receive in school regarding "real life" issues that will help them function in the real world, such as finances. The best thing you can do for your kids is to teach them to manage their finances. Teach them how to balance a checkbook and how to read a bank statement. Teach them to set a goal of saving twenty percent of each paycheck and putting it into a savings account for emergency purposes, such as job loss or unexpected medical expenses. Teach them what interest is and how to use is to their advantage rather than let interest take advantage of them. There is a very disturbing trend among college students who are getting conned into getting their first credit cards and accumulating a lot of debt by the time they graduate.

They start out their adult lives at a disadvantage when they are using their first paychecks from their first jobs just to pay off credit card debt! You can help them establish a credit history of their own by giving them a credit card in their name attached to your account in good standing. A good example of this is an American Express charge card. The balance is due in full every month and you have complete visibility to the monthly statements. Make them accountable for their monthly charges whether it is from an after school job or from an allowance. It gets them in the habit of spending wisely and paying balances off rather than learning to accumulate interest.

I think it's a good idea to set up savings accounts with debit cards for children. We have done this for our kids. They must however maintain a minimum balance of $100.00 in their accounts. They earn money for chores on a bi-monthly basis, similar to how a paycheck is earned. The money is then deposited into their accounts and they look forward to seeing their statements each month. They are learning that the more money that is in their account then the more interest they earn. I have found that if they use their own money then they quickly are able to discern between wants and needs.

It is so important that your children know that they can trust you with anything that might be going on with them, regardless of what it is. So many teens make stupid decisions regarding their personal safety because they become irrational when confronted with a problem. For example, if your teen is caught drinking at a party and decides to drive themselves home because they think, "My parents will kill me if they find out I've been drinking!" the results could be catastrophic. Before those situations arise it is imperative to have conversations with them regarding potential issues where alcohol, cigarettes, drugs or sex is available or might be happening. They need to know that they can call you NO MATTER WHAT and ask for a ride home with a guarantee that you will not discuss it until the next day when you both have had some time to regroup.

I have had this conversation with my oldest daughter and we have an agreement between us. I told her that I remember what it was like to be a teenager, even though it was eons ago. I also told her that she would find herself in situations that she didn't intend to be in. If she feels threatened or uncomfortable in any way she knows that she can call me and I will be there with no questions asked. It also means that I don't automatically assume she is in the wrong because she finds herself in an uncomfortable or inappropriate situation. We have an open line of communication of safety. She also knows that she can use the old line "Sorry I don't do that because my mom would kill me!" I told her that she could always make me out to be the bad guy when necessary!

Another thing to remember is that your children are listening to you even when you think they are not. When confronted with difficult choices regarding peer pressure, your voice will echo in their heads like their conscience. It 's important to teach your children from an early age the importance of CHARACTER. It's even more important to teach them by your example. Remember that they are always watching you.

There are ten character traits that I feel should be taught in every home, as well as in every school. I truly believe that if we all lived our lives by these simple truths then the world would be a better place.

*Honesty - moral uprightness and truthfulness
*Fairness - being fair by being just and impartial
*Responsibility - taking initiative and being responsible for self
*Accountability - taking responsibility for our actions
*Integrity - the possession of firm principles
*Perseverance – determined continuation with something
*Kindness – the ability to behave kindly or with compassion

*Respect – to not go against or violate something and to be considerate
*Trustworthiness - reliable
*Citizenship – good social conduct

I am constantly amazed at the fact that so many parents just assume that somehow their children are going to learn how to become good people without any emphasis on character. Our duty as parents regardless of our race, religion or socio-economic status is to raise our children to become responsible, self-sufficient, morally accountable, socially aware productive members of society.

Focus On Your Family

If you don't make your family a priority then it will never be one. If you don't consciously make a plan to focus on your family then you will blink and before you know it ten years will have passed you by. Don't waste another minute to put your family at the top of your TO DO LIST. There are several things you can do to make the most of the precious time you have with each other. The family that plays together stays together.

Don't make the mistake of over-scheduling your children. So many children are involved in so many different activities that they have obligations at least four evenings a week; therefore, leaving very little time for relaxation. Numerous activities usually mean that the weekends consist of going from one extracurricular activity to another. If you are a working parent then the weekend can seem even more stressful than your workweek! These children are under a tremendous amount of pressure to excel in every activity that they are stressed beyond their limits.

The stress children and teens feel to achieve excellence, even if it is self-inflicted, can lead to dangerous behavior in order to cope such as drug or alcohol abuse or even suicide. It is important as parents to monitor the number of activities that your child is involved in. In our household academics are priorities. They are allowed to compete in one UIL competition per semester as well as one extracurricular activity per semester. I want to ensure that my children have ample study time at home as well as time with the family and time to just relax and be a kid.

If you have more than one child involved in more than one activity each, then I can guarantee that you will spend the majority of their childhood in the car, seldom eat a wholesome meal and rarely will you see your husband. This is a great opportunity to teach your children not to participate in something just for the sake of doing it. It forces them to prioritize and really focus on what they want to participate in and why.

Make one night a week a family night. There are so many different themes that you could come up with. Game night is a fun idea. Take turns letting each member of the family choose what game is going to be played whether it be Monopoly, Scrabble, Charades, etc. The point is to spend the evening together doing something fun and inexpensive at home. Another idea might be to have a family movie night. Order a pizza and gather around the family TV and watch a movie together.

If the weather is cooperative, outdoor activities are great ideas and encourage exercise. Sunday afternoons are great times to go play miniature golf, golf, and tennis or riding bikes together as a family. If it is in your budget, going out to dinner one night a week or for lunch on Sundays is a great idea. Let each member of the family take a turn choosing where to eat. Another fun idea is to establish a restaurant that everyone enjoys and make it a habit of eating there every Thursday evening for example. Simple things like that give each member a little something fun to look forward to each week.

Dinner is a wonderful opportunity to reconnect with each other as a family. I realize that due to extracurricular activities it isn't always possible to gather around the dining room table on a regular basis. However, I would encourage you to make this happen as often as possible. Let your family know that this is a priority in your household. Give each family member the option of choosing the menu one night each week. Set aside one night either weekly or whatever works for your family when you use your good china. Everyone will feel special and it will give them something fun to anticipate. Why is it that we only use the "good dishes" for our company or only on holidays? If your own family isn't good enough use those dishes, then who are?

One of my favorite family traditions is what we call "The Thankful Box." We have a small shoebox that our children decorated that holds special notes from each family member. It started out as a Thanksgiving tradition that turned into a monthly event. At Thanksgiving we have each member of the family write down at least five things that they are grateful for and place them in the box. After our meal we pass the box around and everyone reads someone else's card. I thought that it was such a wonderful way for our family to express our gratitude that I decided to make it a monthly event.

Throughout the month every family member writes down something or someone for which they are grateful and places it in The Thankful Box once a week. At the end of the month we take turns reading one another's expressions of gratitude at dinner. It is an experience that brings our family together and reminds us on a regular basis what is truly important in our lives and to not take anything or anyone for granted and to be grateful for all things.

Another great way to involve each family member is to establish a Vacation Fund. Commit to contributing a certain amount of each paycheck to your fund. Encourage family members to put all of their loose change at the end of the week into the Vacation Fund. You would be amazed at how much loose change adds up to! You might have your family offer three destinations to choose from and once or twice a year draw a destination out of a hat. Spend the entire year planning your trip, making a reservation and researching everything about your vacation. Assign tasks to each family member to research such as available activities, weather trends, local hot spots, accommodations, demographics and diversified food options. The point is to get everyone involved and excited about the adventure.

People are living longer lives and this puts a strain on society in almost every way. As our population increases, so does the strain on our natural resources as well as our social resources exponentially. Social Security is in jeopardy and most likely won't be available to those of us who pay into it by the time we reach sixty-five and there are record numbers of uninsured people everywhere. The dynamics of "retirement" have changed for almost everyone and forced us to rethink and reorganize our plans for our futures.

In many cases this means that we might be caring for our elderly parents due to the cost of healthcare, dwindling 401k accounts and pension funds. If you find yourself in this situation then you are faced with two options: you can either embrace it or resent it. I have been in this situation and my recommendation is to choose to embrace it. Having a parent or grandparent become a part of your own family can really be a very rewarding experience for everyone.

There are many cultures that have multiple generations residing under one roof. There is a cohesive environment in which all members work together for the success of the entire family. Elders are respected and participate in raising the children. Of course this is very different than our society and I realize that the idea of your mother in law helping in the daily decisions regarding child rearing might seem less than appealing.

If you become responsible for the care of an elder then there are initial steps to take in order to make a smooth transition for all involved. Regardless of the circumstances the first decision to be made is where the parent in need will reside. If it is in your family's budget, assisted living facilities are a wonderful solution. They usually provide transportation, all meals, an on-site RN, laundry services and activities. They also provide residents with independence via private rooms so that they can participate as much or as little as they want to and still go "home" to their own rooms. There are many different assisted living facilities that vary in price range. Take the time to do the research and take tours of these facilities in your area. They allow you to still be involved in your loved one's life as often as you want to be without the actual burden of daily maintenance.

However, due to cost or circumstance this might not be an option for you and your parent might need to live with you. The first thing to due in this scenario is for you and your husband to decide what "role" your parent will be playing in your family. Boundaries need to be established regarding all dynamics that make up your family. Once you and your husband have made those decisions you need to have that same conversation with your parent before they move in. For example, will your parent be expected to be present at all meals or will they eat some meals on their own time? Will your parent be doing their own laundry or will you be doing it for them? If they are capable and expected to do their own laundry, then they need to know what day is their designated day, etc…

Your parent also needs to clearly understand what the boundaries are concerning your children. If there are topics that you don't want them discussing with your children then you need to be very specific about what those are. Your parent needs to be supportive of your discipline and consequence policies whether or not they agree with them. They should never be allowed to negate your authority in your own home or negotiate on your children's behalf. Children are brilliant at using the divide and conquer philosophy. Many times they will use both parents against the other to get the answer they want. If mom says no then they'll go ask dad. If your children understand that you and your husband present a united front then they will realize that this tactic is useless.

The most important part of coexisting with your parent and making it work is to be flexible. Realize how vulnerable your parent is feeling and be sensitive to the fact that they might be feeling helpless. Look for signs of depression and make their doctor aware of these symptoms if they present themselves. It is very difficult transitioning from being the parent to needing to be parented in a sense. Many seniors feel like a burden to their children and often feel useless. It's important for them to feel like a part of your family and that their presence is valued in your home. There are some simple things you can do to achieve this.

Smile whenever they walk into the room and greet them with affection. They often feel like children waking up from a nap whenever they walk into your space. They will be timid and are looking for reassurance that it's all right for them to be there. Make them feel welcome, even if they are an inconvenience. Don't take your frustrations out on them; vent in private and NEVER in front of your children.

Your family will follow your lead dealing with your parent living with you. If you are resentful and negative then they will be too. However, if you approach this situation as an opportunity to grow as a family then they will be open minded to your approach. If your parent eats dinner with you then include them in the conversation. Children can learn so much from elders. Elders can be a wealth of information about history and life experience.

I helped care for my grandfather who was legally blind after my grandmother died. I was very close to them both and I was glad to be able to give back to him what I felt he had given me throughout my life. All of my children were fortunate enough to be able to spend a lot of time with him and they enjoyed a wonderful relationship with a remarkable man. One of my fondest memories is when my middle daughter took my grandfather to "Show and Tell" in first grade. He told the students about crashing in an airplane and surviving during World War II. It was an experience that both my daughter and my grandfather cherished.

Research all of the senior services in your community. There are so many different resources available if you are willing to look. There are elder day care programs that offer assistance for a couple of hours or longer if needed, especially if you work during the day and are unable to care for your parent full time. Talk with you parent's physician regarding what Medicare will and won't pay for. Visit your community center and find out what programs are available at Senior Centers that offer various activities to participate in. There are also some programs that offer "Adopt a Grandparent" services that involve volunteers committing to spending a certain amount of time with seniors weekly, which are similar to the Big Brothers Big Sisters programs. Investigate various senior transportation services through charitable organizations that can help ease your burden on your family.

Look for support groups that you can join with people experiencing similar circumstances. Support groups are wonderful resources and offer varied points of view and help. Realize that your situation is only temporary and understand that someday you may also find yourself in the same situation your parent is in. Handle yourself in a manner that will ensure you will have no regrets in the future.

With the average divorce rate in our society at around fifty percent, it is likely that many people are dealing with a blended family situation where there are either stepparents or stepsiblings or both involved. This is a very powerful and often very stressful dynamic. Everyone approaches family situations with their own circumstances and experiences. The goal should be to combine our experiences and form a cohesive unit that has the family's best interests in mind.

I have interviewed many stepparents, I had stepparents of my own and my husband is a stepparent to my three daughters. Most of these people all shared a common thread…they said that it was very hard not to take what their stepchildren either said or did personally. When you enter into a marriage where you will become a stepparent, it is easy to feel like you are automatically at a deficit because you don't have the bond of blood binding you to each other. It's important to keep in mind that blood doesn't necessarily make you a family, but love always does.

Everyone's experiences will differ depending on the age of the stepchildren as well as the status of the relationship between former spouses. My parents exhibited a great example to me of how two people who were divorced could maintain a very amicable relationship and always put my needs ahead of their differences. I feel very fortunate to have such wonderful parents and a wonderful stepmother. However, my ex husband has demonstrated the opposite end of the spectrum of grace and decorum, unlike my parents and therefore, forced us all to see the worst possible outcome of a divorce for everyone involved. I feel like I am very well versed in most scenarios.

Whether you are the natural parent or the stepparent you should avoid making disparaging remarks about the other natural parent or the stepparent in front of the children. One thing that adults forget is that children are made up of both parents and when they hear something negative about one of their parents it makes them feel badly about themselves because they know that they are a part of that parent and identify with them in some way. Even if the other parent isn't deserving of praise, keep your negative commentary to yourself for the sake of the children.

Bitterly divorced parents often use their children as pawns in order to hurt one another. What they seldom realize in the heat of the moment due to their blind rage and hatred for the other person is that the only people who actually get hurt are the children. It might take years but eventually those children end up resenting the parent who was constantly trying to turn them against the other parent.

If your children have extracurricular activities or obligations that interferes with the scheduled visitation, be open minded to being flexible for the sake of your children. Don't demand that they spend the scheduled weekend with you in order to prove that you are in charge, especially if there is significant distance involved. As a parent it is important to put your child's happiness above your own agenda. Does it really make sense to have your children spend the better part of every other weekend either traveling on a plane or in a car for the sake of scheduled visitation? Offer to switch weekends to accommodate your child's schedule or offer to spend more time with them during the summer and let them know that the things that are going on in their life are important to you. The worst thing you could do would be to put unnecessary stress on your child by demanding that you get your visitation or by telling them that because they are children that their activities are irrelevant.

As the biological parent it is important that you help your children see their stepparent's point of view. At the same time it is also important for you help your spouse who is a stepparent see your children's point of view as well. For example, a stepparent and a stepchild might interpret a stepchild's messy room differently. A stepparent might see a messy room as a sign of disrespect for not taking care of the home that is provided for them whereas a stepchild simply might have not made cleaning up a priority rather than meaning to be disrespectful.

Misinterpreted dialogue is also a potential problem. As parents we can usually take any off the cuff remarks our children make and shrug them off. This might not be so easy for a stepparent to do. A child usually doesn't differentiate between parent and stepparent when expressing their displeasure to a certain topic of discussion. However, it is important that you help the stepparent understand that your child would say the exact same thing to you and that it truly isn't personal. You also need to express to your child that they should exercise sensitivity when vocalizing frustrations whether it is with words or with the familiar sighs and groans and emphasize that it could potentially be hurtful. The point is for both of them to be sensitive to one another's points of view and be able to communicate. If you are the biological parent then it is your job to be the mediator and help make communication easy.

If your child's other biological parent is getting remarried it is important for you to be supportive of the marriage.

Your children will look to you to see how to react. If you are bitter and resentful then you will only strain the relationship your child will inevitably have with the new stepparent. Remember that whether you like them or not this new person will be a large part of your child's life. If you can be positive about the marriage and help your child see the importance of their other biological parent finding happiness it will help your child to feel better about the union.

The dumbest thing that you could do would be to make an enemy of someone who will have an influence over your child, even if it is only part time. Realize that you will be partners with this person in sharing the raising of your children and help them to make a smooth transition with your children. Encourage your children to be accepting of the new parent in their lives and try to help them focus on that person's attributes. The new parent will appreciate your support and be much more open to the idea of loving your children. Otherwise your children will become very unattractive to their stepparent. Don't view the new parent as competition. Realize that you can't be replaced and be grateful for the addition of another person to love your child.

Just like two biological parents raising a child together it is also important for a biological parent and a stepparent to present a united front in regards to the children. Don't allow them to try to use you against the other parent with the tired old saying, "I don't have to mind you because you're not my real mom or my real dad!" Children need to understand from the very beginning that it is pointless to try to divide their parents for their own gain. Don't allow any guilt you might be feeling about putting a child through a divorce to influence you by giving in to your child's every whim for fear of resentment.

Children are great manipulators if you allow them to be. What children need the most is consistency in all areas of their lives. They need you to be consistent with the love and praise you give them as well as with your discipline and expectations. Whether they admit it or not they want and need boundaries. By understanding the consequences of their actions you are helping your children acquire the tools they will need to carry them into adulthood.

Teach your children that their hearts are expandable like balloons. Show them that the more love they fill their hearts with, the larger their heart becomes; therefore, allowing enough room in their hearts for everyone in their lives.

The love of a stepparent is truly the most special kind of love because it is chosen. They love without obligation because they choose to, not because they have to. Stepparents can often offer a truly objective perspective to almost any situation because they don't have on those "mother or father goggles" which sometimes prevent us from seeing reality. There will also be those times when your children may not feel comfortable talking to you about something BECAUSE you are the biological parent. If you establish good lines of communication that will lead to trust, hopefully your child will turn to their stepparent for counsel when they feel like they can't come to you. Everyone wins in that situation because you know that your child will be getting advice from someone that you both love and trust and has your child's best interest in mind.

Families are like marriages. They take work. They don't just happen. However, there is nothing more rewarding than a cohesive family who knows that they are solid and have one another's backs.

Learn To Say "No!"

I'm not exactly sure at what age it begins that most females want to become pleasers. For whatever reason we don't want anyone to be upset with us, even if it means that we are inconvenienced. It is amazing to think of all the things we as women say "Yes" to that we really don't want. It's as if by saying "No" that we are somehow admitting defeat or failure. There are so many women and mothers afflicted with what I refer to as the "martyr syndrome." There are a lot of women out there that believe if they put themselves last and take on excessive responsibilities then other people will admire them for their selflessness. The truth of the matter is… no one else is watching or even cares. Those women only set themselves up for failure.

There are and will always be those women that everyone knows are the "go to" people when everyone else says no. These are also the very same people who have "DOORMAT" stamped on their foreheads. Just because you let everyone walk all over you doesn't make you Mother Teresa; it just makes you stupid. People don't respect the person who never says no, they simply take advantage of them.

How many times have you told the person on the other end of the phone that you would be glad to chair the PTA Fundraiser when you had absolutely no idea how you were going to manage that project on top of everything else that you were committed to? We've all done it at least once or twice. We agree to something we either don't want to do or can't possibly manage and regret it the very instant we hang up the phone. The next thing you know you are burning the candle at both ends and making everyone in your life, including yourself, miserable.

Remember that you have a lifetime to volunteer and participate in charitable organizations. There is no unwritten rule that says you must say yes to everyone who asks you for help. Rather than agreeing to chair an event that you know will take over your life, offer to participate on a smaller scale. Tell the inquirer that you would be able to volunteer three hours on the day of the event or be able to bake some cookies instead, but that due to previous commitments you won't be able to chair the entire event. I promise that you will earn more respect by being honest about your availability than by over extending yourself.

When you get the guilt tripping phone call from your minister asking you to teach the Kindergarten Sunday school class for the entire year because Mrs. Brown is having hip replacement surgery, try this approach: Rather than saying yes because you feel obligated, politely take a deep breath and say, "Rev. Smith, I wish I could commit to teaching every Sunday, but that would put too much of a strain on my family; however, I could perhaps fill in one Sunday each month instead. If several other families could do the same thing then your problem would be solved." If you aren't sure of what to say, simply reply, "I will have to discuss this with my family and get back to you in a couple of days." This will allow you time to actually assess the situation and find out what if any capacity you would be capable of helping. We all get ourselves in trouble by panicking and answering before we've actually had a chance to think realistically about it.

We spend so much wasted time trying to please people that really don't affect our lives in one way or the other in the big scheme of things. The tragedy is that because we get caught up in that vicious cycle we often disappoint the only people who should matter to us because we put them last... our families. There is no grand prize at the end of this life for having the most volunteer hours racked up or for belonging to the most organizations or being on the board of fifty different organizations. The only thing that truly matters at the end of your life is that you were honorable to the people you really have an obligation to and that is yourself and your family.

I firmly believe in the mantra that in order to lead we must first learn to serve. I think that your children should witness you giving back to your community and volunteering to help those less fortunate; however, not at their expense. When it is appropriate you should involve your children in charity so that they don't grow up with a skewed perspective of how the world revolves. Teach them to take care of themselves and the planet and to not be wasteful of anything, including their time, food, money or natural resources. Time is something that we can never get back and all of the wishing in the world won't change it. Invest your time wisely where you can make an actual difference and for the right reasons.

Your children are watching everything that you do. Set a good example for them by placing value in yourself and your time and your family's time. Teach them to be selective about their commitments. It will keep them from piling on unnecessary stress onto themselves. Stress is one of the most insidious stalkers of our existence. It is also one of the most avoidable. Most of the stress in our lives is self-induced and therefore, avoidable.

Sometimes we need to re-evaluate the people in our lives and determine whether or not they are good for our family and us. I relate it to a yearly performance review. Circumstances and situations change...so do people. If a friend betrays you then you should cut them loose. Betrayals come in many different forms and it doesn't matter what type of a betrayal it was. You do not need someone in your life that gossips about you behind your back, sabotages you or flirts with your husband. This decision will require no explanation on your part. However, if you find that silence is not effective and your "friend" demands to know why you won't return her calls then tell her. Explain in your gentlest tone that you are a genuine person and that there is no room in your life for unauthentic people. Simply clean house of the trash in your life and move on.

Get Organized

Abraham Lincoln had this approach to the work ethic…"If I had six hours to chop down a tree, I would spend four hours sharpening the axe." The reason we feel overwhelmed most of the time is because we don't have a clearly defined plan of attack and we are poorly prepared. Most of us just wing it and hope we manage to get everything done without forgetting too much in the process. If you learn to organize all aspects of your life then the natural rhythm of life is less interrupted and doesn't feel as daunting.

If you are organized in all areas of your life then you are removing the variables that can potentially cause you trouble. You will be better equipped to handle the emergencies that will inevitably arise that are beyond your control when you have a firm grasp on everything else. I suggest making a pie chart of the areas in your life that need to be organized. These will be different for everyone. I'm not a mathematician and I don't expect you to be one either. Simply use my suggestions as a guide to fill in the blanks of your own life. If you look at your pie chart like a pizza, then you will realize that if one piece is missing it isn't a whole pizza.

One of the first areas to organize is your financial piece of the pie. Nothing will put a larger strain on your marriage or your family like disorganized finances. It's important to sit down with your husband and make a realistic budget. It's even more important to stick to it. If you are like millions of other families who are drowning in a sea of debt, then I suggest you make a plan to get out of it. If you are able to get a debt consolidation loan, that is a faster way to pay down your debt with a more realistic interest rate. Operate on a "cash only" basis and put up your credit cards. Keep them for emergency use only or for traveling. If you do use your credit cards, then pay off your balance each month in order to avoid paying high interest rates.

If you aren't able to get a debt consolidation loan, then commit to putting as much as you possibly can each month toward your credit card debt. When you only make the minimum required payments you are locking yourself into an eternal prison of debt with little hope of ever getting out. Try to at least double or triple the minimum payments each month and stick to it. You will slowly but surely see your balances start to dwindle. It is important at this time to exercise fiscal restraint by being able to differentiate between WANTS and NEEDS.

If you don't have a filing cabinet I strongly recommend getting one. Create a file for every bill that goes out each month and keep your statements in it for backup. Keep a current "Tax Information" file for your current year's taxes. Tax time will be less intimidating if you can retrieve your information with all of your deductible expenses and income information located in one place. I also think it is a good idea to input your monthly financial information into your computer on a financial software program such as Microsoft Money or QuickBooks. You will be able to keep track of your spending by printing out monthly reports to see exactly where each dollar goes.

Scheduling maintenance is one of the simplest things you can do to improve the quality of your life and avoid unnecessary and sometimes costly emergencies. Poor maintenance can lead to expensive repairs across the board. Change the oil in your vehicles on a regular basis and rotate and balance your tires as often as is recommended due to the amount of your driving time. Schedule whatever maintenance is required per mileage according to your owner's manual.

Pay attention to your tire pressure as seasons change and correct it as needed. Little things can greatly improve your gas mileage. Put these things on your calendar and make a point to follow it. It may sound like a no brainer but you would be amazed at the number of people who pay little attention to the very vehicle that they depend on to safely transport their families every day. Wash your car and vacuum the interior at least once every two weeks, but preferably once a week. Psychologically, driving a clean and well maintained car will make you feel better about having to be in it so often.

Change your air filters in your home regularly. Depending on where you live might determine the frequency in which you replace them. Due to the fact that we have two family members with severe allergies, we choose to replace our filters once a month. Poor air quality in the home can create difficult breathing situations for your family such as allergies and asthma. Minimize the use of curtains and carpet in your home wherever possible. They are dust magnets and almost impossible to keep clean.

A clean home is a healthy home. Whether you do it yourself or hire someone to do it for you, it is important to clean your home on a regular basis. It is probably your largest asset. I am often amazed at how poorly people care for something that they worked so hard to attain! At least once a week there are certain things that should be done: bed linens should be washed, bathrooms should be thoroughly cleaned and floors should be vacuumed and mopped.

If someone else is coming into your home, don't assume that they are cleaning to your specifications. Clearly line out your desired cleaning requirements and make sure they are being met. Remember that your family's health depends on it. However, if you are cleaning your own home then I recommend setting a schedule for yourself. It is almost impossible to accomplish all of the necessary tasks in one day each week. For example, you might decide that Mondays are for cleaning bathrooms and Tuesdays are dusting and vacuuming days. The point is to set realistic goals for your home and make sure they are getting met. This is a good opportunity to get your children involved in the maintenance of the home that they live in. Chances are that they will minimize their messes if they will be helping in cleaning them also.

Laundry should be scheduled the same way you schedule cleaning the house. Depending on the size of your family you can customize your laundry routine. There are six people in our home; therefore, laundry is done every single day it seems. I have my three oldest children separate their laundry and send laundry baskets upstairs with them. I usually designate one day for whites, one day for colors, one day for bed linens, etc. Of course this changes with the needs of our family, but it's a place to start as well as a guarantee that the laundry doesn't pile up and become insurmountable.

Clean out each family member's closets each quarter. Donate outgrown clothes and unused items in your home to your favorite charitable organization. Put your receipt in your "tax info." folder. If you are brave enough to tackle a garage sale, then you can get together with other neighbors quarterly and split the advertising costs. You can make a lot of money at a garage sale if the items you are selling are in good condition and your "booth" is well organized. Your vacation fund might be a good place to put your garage sale profits or you might use your proceeds towards a large needed family purchase.

Teach your family to recycle and make a recycling schedule whether it includes having your recyclables picked up or involves you taking your recyclables to your local recycling plant. Keep recycling bins clearly labeled in the garage and use them on a daily basis. Help your children learn to make responsible choices regarding recycled material.

I plan weekly meals for my family. I have found that it reduces the stress of trying to come up with an idea for a meal each and every day. This is also very helpful with the grocery shopping. It greatly reduces the need to make unnecessary trips to the supermarket for one or two items to complete a meal. It is almost impossible to adhere to your grocery budget if you are making several trips to the store each week.

We often feel compelled to make our trip "worthwhile" so we buy extra items that aren't needed in order look as though we intended to be at the store. If each additional trip to the grocery adds up to an extra twenty to thirty dollars that wasn't necessary then it will be impossible to stick to your budget. By being organized about meal choices and shopping in an efficient manner you will be amazed at your potential savings. I also encourage you to print coupons online or clip them in your newspaper. Be aware of your in store specials and shop accordingly. Strive to make each dollar spend like ten dollars.

The outside of your home is as important as the inside of your home. Don't neglect things like your lawn, shrubs and trim that need to be painted. A safe policy to practice is to fix problems as they occur. If projects continually get postponed then nothing ever gets fixed and the "to do list" gets so long and expensive that it becomes impossible to manage. The bottom line is to take pride in your home. A well maintained home that is run efficiently reduces the stress level on families and allows them to focus on each other rather than focusing on all of the needed maintenance without a clear plan of attack.

Some men are not born with the aptitude required to fix things around the house. There are also those who have the ability but lack the motivation. If either scenario applies to you then it is worth your while to either take a class designed for women wanting to learn to manage repairs around the home or to invest in the services of a handyman. If you are hiring someone to come into your home, make sure that you check their references and their status with the Better Business Bureau. It is important to hire a professional rather than a scam artist. Take your personal safety and the safety of your home very seriously and don't be too trusting.

Always be skeptical. If you start out with skepticism then everything positive that you find out will be a pleasant surprise.

It is also important to take care of your physical being as well. If you are able to do nothing else, at least commit to walking for thirty minutes at least three times a week. Getting fresh air and exercise on a regular basis is essential to a good quality of life. By engaging in physical activity you will also improve your mental outlook as well. If you can incorporate even more exercise into your weekly routine then that would be even better. Remember that your body is a gift and that it has to last your entire lifetime. Be good to it and it will be good to you.

Emotional health is vital to your existence. Your emotions affect everything that you say and do. It is necessary for you to find a few moments for yourself each day to simply sit in silence and reflect on your state of mind. For me the very best time of the day to find some peace is before everyone else in the house is awake. I allow myself at least fifteen minutes of complete silence where I clear my mind and organize my thoughts. This is also the time that I choose to pray for my day ahead. It clears my perspective on all that I need to do and be responsible for. Prayer is a personal choice, but meditation or whatever spirit renewing exercise you choose will do. I like to think of my quiet time as a way for me to "clean the slate" in order to start the day fresh and energized.

I have also found that it is very important for me to continue to learn by reading a variety of information. Otherwise, I feel as though my mind is turning to mush. I make a point to spend at least thirty minutes each evening reading something of value or of interest to me. I strive to continually expand my vocabulary and range of knowledge each week and have encouraged my children to do the same. I never want to stop learning in life, even if I am no longer in school.

Once you have the physical and emotional aspects of your pie organized it is important to get your spiritual slice in order. It doesn't matter what your religious beliefs are, if you believe in a higher power or higher being it is important to be in touch with your spirit on a daily basis. Whether it is through prayer or meditation, give yourself a center each day to launch from and to run to.

Children learn by example and if they observe you relying on your spirituality to ground you and help you get through life's trials then they will also learn to be in tune with their spirituality as well. Whenever possible worship together as a family. It might mean praying together before a meal or attending a weekly worship service. Talk openly about your faith with your children. Guide their moral compass and give them the tools to make spiritual decisions. Don't allow other people to influence your children's spirituality that you might not approve of.

Prepare for your next day the night before. For example, make sure that you end the day with a clean kitchen and get the coffee ready for the following morning. Even something as trivial as preparing a pot of coffee at 6:00 a.m. can seem utterly difficult. If you couple that with a sink full of dirty dishes you might end up deciding to just go back to bed and forget about it! Make either a mental or physical list of what needs to be done the next day. Select your clothes so that it is one less decision needing to be made in the morning. Pack your car the night before so you don't forget something as you are rushing out the door. You will sleep better knowing that you have a less stressful start to the day ahead of you.

By being organized in all areas of your life you reduce the occurrence of surprises. There will always be those things that are impossible to anticipate, but if you can eliminate as many variables as possible you will be better equipped to deal when them as they arise.

Handle Adversity With Grace

It is inevitable that we will all lose our cool at one time or another and think that we could have handled a certain situation much better and with a little more class. The point is to not make a habit of feeling that way and making it our reality. I firmly believe that grace is the ability to understand that whenever a crisis arises to have the presence of mind to also realize that it shall also pass. Nothing is ever quite as bad as it seems and is most always temporary.

One of the worst things you can ever do is to panic in front of your children. They need stability above all else. If you need to freak out then do it in private. If they overhear a stressful phone call try to reassure them that everything is okay and fall apart in your bathroom. Put on a brave front for the sake of their sanity. We often believe what we say aloud and if we are speaking calmly and rationally then we can convince ourselves that everything will be okay and talk ourselves through an anxiety attack.

Giving in to the opportunity of a nervous breakdown is always a bad idea. Nothing productive ever comes of it. When you always expect the worst to happen, it usually does. Plan your day in advance and see it unfolding the way you want it to. Many times our despair becomes a self-fulfilling prophecy. Try not to fall asleep dwelling on the day's problems or disappointments. Those thoughts are a toxic environment for your mind to swim around in. If you drift off to sleep in misery it is difficult to wake up optimistic and therefore productive.

There is nothing more unattractive than someone who lacks the ability to cope with the daily rhythm of life. Things go awry and things get broken. Expecting perfection is unrealistic. We all have to be able to adapt to change as well as cope with the unexpected. If you are under the impression that you are the only person in the world who things go wrong for, then you are sorely mistaken and you probably make those around you completely insane. It is so frustrating to listen to someone ramble on and on about EVERYTHING that has ever gone wrong in their life for because they got a flat tire! Who doesn't know someone who always reacts with complete irrationality with comments such as, "This kind of thing only happens to me! Nothing ever goes my way!" whenever a problem arises?

Those people often have little credibility with others and usually just get ignored by everyone. While they are busy having a tirade the rest of us are thinking, "Yeah right pal, you're not the only one who has problems just the only one who can't cope!" Slow and steady is always the best policy in almost every situation. Never underestimate the power of patience. Most of our mistakes are made in haste without thought of consequence. If we allow ourselves the opportunity to calmly navigate our way through difficulty then we can usually avoid the choppy waters in the process.

There is never an excuse for you to raise your voice. I have found that when conversations become escalated it is easier to diffuse them by demonstrating the opposite reaction. The louder someone around you begins to talk, the quieter you should speak. They will inevitably have to lower their volume just to hear you; therefore, calming down whether they want to or not. It is very difficult to argue or fight with someone who refuses to engage in battle. Nothing will ever get solved in the heat of the moment when nerves are raw and emotions are out of control. Handle yourself with class at all times and resist the temptation to lower your standards, even if it means walking away temporarily.

Whenever you are experiencing a moment of crisis that makes your blood pressure rise, immediately take a moment to center yourself and take several deep breaths. Square your shoulders and hold your head high and believe that you will find a solution. If you simply put pen to paper and make a list of pros and cons in your life then most of the time you will determine that you have much more in the positive column. It is just easier to stay mad or frustrated if we are only focusing the negatives. Why is it that we want to hold on to anger? How many times have you said to yourself in the middle of a heated moment, "I can't believe I am this upset over something so trivial and allowed myself to say that." It is like the snowball effect. Once something is set in motion it can be very difficult to either slow down or stop.

Don't paint a doom and gloom picture of the world for your children to see. Someone very close to me told me that when he was a very young child his mother told him that the world was a terrible place and he should just get used to it. Wow. Can you imagine the person whom you are supposed to most respect and admire just taking the wind out of you sails like that? She turned out to be a lousy example on all fronts! As adults we become cynical based on our experiences. Your children deserve the right to look at the world with optimism and hope. Prejudice is learned and so is pessimism. Why burden anyone with something so negative? If every time you face adversity you display utter despair then your children will never learn how to cope with strife that will inevitably come their way.

However, if you face adversity with dignity, levelheadedness, grace and gumption then your family will never drown in a sea of despair. More importantly, you will not continue to worsen the situation by surrounding yourself with such negativity. Pessimism breeds depression and depression leads to stress and illness, which are all counterproductive.

I'm not saying that you should live in denial. Whenever adversity rears its head the most important step in getting through the crisis is acceptance. Once you accept your situation then you can start to find a way out of it or at least through it. Remember, "Adversity doesn't build character, it reveals it." What does the adversity in your life reveal about you? What do you WANT it to reveal?

Epilogue

At the beginning of the book I asked you if you had any ideas of what the success of your family meant to you. I hope that after the reading you have discovered what success means on your own terms by incorporating some of the suggested ideas.

Through the journey of writing this book I rediscovered that there are no greater gifts in my life beyond those of my marriage and my children. I am reminded through circumstance that my life and my roles as wife and mother will always be a work in progress. As long as I continue to strive to be the person I was intended to be then I am always moving forward on this miraculous journey of life. Sometimes we take steps backwards and sometimes we even fall. The important thing to remember is to pick yourself up and continue to move forward each and every day.

I hope that you have found a new appreciation for yourself and your family as well as the confidence to try something new. Remember that we only get one chance to raise our families and that those experiences will last them a lifetime. My goal for anyone who took the time to read this book is that you will be reinvigorated about your life and excited about what lies ahead for your family. To quote Abraham Lincoln one last time, "And in the end, it's not the years in your life that count. It's the life in your years." My best to you!